Making Education Work
How Black men and boys navigate the Further Education sector

Making Education Work
How Black men and boys navigate the Further Education sector

Sheine Peart

A Trentham Book
Institute of Education Press, London

Institute of Education Press
20 Bedford Way
London
WC1H 0AL

First published 2013

British Library Cataloguing-in-Publication Data
A catalogue record for this book is available from the British Library

ISBN 978-1-85856-509-5

The publishers would like to thank Luke for the photos from his family album

Printed by CPI Group (UK) Ltd, Croydon, CR0 4YY

Contents

Dedication

*This book is dedicated to all the boys and men
who took part in this study and all those who are currently
on the Black on Track project*

Acknowledgments

I am a big advocate of TEAM, an acronym for Together Everyone Achieves More. I am grateful to have been part of a team whose collective efforts enabled me to write this book.

Particular thanks are extended to the academic team who guided me along the way, Morwenna Griffiths, Tony Cotton, Roy Corden, Sue Wallace, Rob Dransfield, Peter Clough, Keith Dennis, Mal Cowgill and Cecile Wright. I am truly grateful for their untiring support and guidance. I also want to express my sincere gratitude to all the Black men and boys who so willingly, openly and candidly engaged in this inquiry. Special thanks is reserved for my family: my Mum; my late Dad who is no longer around and who would have so enjoyed reading this book; my brothers Icah and Lance and my late brother Adrian, whose journeys began my thinking; my husband Neil and my son Ben. You are and remain my source of inspiration and strength. Last, but not least, I would like to thank Gillian Klein, who took a chance on me and encouraged me to write this book.

PART ONE
CONTEXTUAL OVERVIEW

1
Setting the scene

Introduction

Within the UK there is a 'broad understanding of equality ... (which) informs many state systems of schooling' (Terzi, 2008:1). Further, 'the dominant understanding of educational equality in contemporary Anglo-American political discourse is meritocratic' (Brighouse, Tooley and Howe, 2010:27) and these same 'liberal, democratic, meritocratic ideals' (Wright, Standen and Patel, 2010:117) dictate it is a student's abilities which should determine their experience of and success within the education system. However, while there appears to be an acceptance of the principle of equality in education, not all groups are able to access education in the same way or enjoy a similar experience of education. Some groups, it seems, are positively disadvantaged by the education system. Gillborn argues that inequalities are so structurally ingrained within the UK education system that failure and marginalisation of some groups is 'inevitable and permanent under current circumstances' (2008:45). Black students appear to be one such group, experiencing both academic underachievement and a hostile social environment, a system which is 'favourable towards one race against another' (Ouseley in Byfield, 2008:x); a system which systematically disadvantages Black learners through 'structural inequalities in schooling' (John, 2010, *Guardian* online).

In her research, Rhamie found that 'most Black children face negative experiences at school' and 'this was found to be true for all groups of every level of attainment' (2007:12). Gillborn adds further weight to this argument when he highlights that White students of the same gender and socio-economic location 'are more likely to succeed than their peers from Pakistani, Bangladeshi, Black Caribbean, Black African, Black Other and Dual Heritage (White/

Black Caribbean) backgrounds' (2008:56). He demonstrates that academic success at secondary school has been predicated on ethnic origin rather than capability, and virtually *all* ethnic minority groups in the same school environments are likely to do less well than their White counterparts, thus confirming earlier research by Coard (1971), Swann (1985), Gillborn and Mirza (2003), the London Development Agency (2004) and Tikly *et al* (2006).

When considering Black students' social interactions in schools, research indicated a similarly challenging picture for Black men and boys. In her research Rhamie also found that Black students regularly experienced negative

> interactions with teachers and staff which (left) them feeling that they (had) been treated differently or unfairly compared to other children. They also (found) a general lack of encouragement from teachers as well as negative, sometimes racist interaction with other children. (2007:12)

The causes of this situation are multiple and complex. However an education system which is organised on an 'unspoken assumption of White-as-norm' (Jensen, 2011:21) in which systems and structures are organised 'from the perspective of White people' (*ibid*:27) and imagines provision for the White community is suitable for *all* communities is unlikely to realise a goal of equality. To achieve educational equality would necessarily mean recognising and providing for difference so that all learners had 'an equal chance to develop and fulfil personal interests and talents' (Terzi, 2008:1).

Unhelpful and damaging stereotypes of Black men and boys characterise them by their 'toughness, sexual promiscuity, manipulation, thrill-seeking and a willingness to use violence to resolve interpersonal conflict' (Majors and Billson, 1992:34). These are characteristics which can hinder success in a system which demands compliance and the willingness to follow direction. However, it is important for those working within education to remember

> Black boys are not a homogenous group. Contrary to popular view, they are not synonymous with underachievement. Many do achieve academically yet the press is littered with headlines about the underachievement of Black boys and a plethora of academic research focuses on the negative outcomes of their schooling. This persistent deficit model reinforces negative stereotypes and adversely affects their expectations, creating a self-fulfilling prophecy. (Byfield, 2008:3)

In this book I look beyond the negative encounters and academic failure of Black men and boys in the statutory sector and consider what happens to this group once they enter further education (FE).

Building on previous work (for example Sewell, 1997, 2004, 2009; Blair, 2001; Rhamie, 2007; Byfield, 2008) I explore whether Black men and boys have a different experience of education when they are in a different learning environment and whether this different environment has the capacity to produce other educational outcomes. This book is for all teachers, trainers and educators working in colleges, schools and other education settings who are interested in and committed to making a difference to the academic success of Black men and boys and who believe that failure is not a predetermined inevitability. It is for teachers who are willing to try new approaches and who want to be part of a change to promote the educational achievement of Black men and boys.

Why this book has been written

Asijeuliza, hanalo ajifunzalo
Those that do not ask questions have nothing to learn (Swahili Proverb)
(Farsi, 1981:5)

My book has a very personal beginning, originating from the questions and confusions that have followed me throughout my interactions as a student and a teacher in primary, secondary and post-compulsory education. Was my Dad right, when he located his sons' difficult relationship with education as entirely a creation of their making? Why were two of my brothers continually at odds with the education system, to the point that neither of them could leave compulsory education quickly enough? Why did this also seem to be the experience of many of my male cousins? Why did Friday afternoon at primary school appear to be a parade of Black boys walking to the headteacher's office to receive punishment for assorted usually unknown misdemeanours? How did so many Black boys manage to end up on the wrong side of discipline systems in both primary and secondary schools? What was happening to create these situations? Was this same experience replicated in the FE sector? Most importantly what did the Black youths themselves think about these different situations and what were their perceptions of these circumstances?

All these questions were significant in forming my thinking and remain important for many Black men and boys as they move through the various education sectors. In this book I focus on one aspect of the learning experience of Black men and boys and consider what happens once they enter FE. My principal research question is: how do Black men and boys perceive and experience education in FE? I have strived to provide alternative perspectives for some of the many unanswered questions and to offer new insights to inform the thinking of other contemporary educators.

The book provides a vehicle for Black men and boys, who have so often experienced a negative relationship with education, an opportunity to tell their personal stories of the daily realities of being a Black man or boy in FE, and in doing so puts 'back the voices that were left out' (Levy, 2010:318). Much writing, including education texts describing the experiences of Black people are 'written by White people with different viewpoints' (*ibid*:319). This book makes a contribution to addressing this omission and through the stories the Black men and boys generously shared with me, I have 'laid bare'(Clough, 2002:5) new understandings of their journey through the post-compulsory sector. It acts an instrument for Black men and boys who took part in this inquiry to provide their 'very individual understanding of events' (Levy, 2010: 321) and to 'sing their songs' (Angelou, 2001:5) in their own words. It is a vehicle which has enabled Black men and boys to speak directly to tutors, teachers and managers 'without 'othering' or exploiting them or leaving them voiceless in the telling of their own stories' (Liamputtong, 2007:165).

Important definitions
Certain key terms are repeatedly used in the book. For clarity I now provide definitions for each of these terms.

Boys and men
In the UK, the word 'boy' generally refers to a male who is below the age of majority, 18. Within a master/slave relationship 'boy' was often used to describe any male slave regardless of their age arising from the assumed superiority of slave owners to slaves and assigning child-like characteristics (naivety, lack of knowledge and understanding) to those so described. In a master/slave context 'boy' was used to describe both child and adult male slaves as a derogatory term. Because of the historical slave association within contemporary society, 'boy' has become a term of insult when used to describe males over the age of about 14. Within a FE context, acknowledging colleges have their roots in an adult learner tradition, 'boy' is not a commonly used term and even younger males would more usually described as young men. Within the context of this study and in order to differentiate between younger and older males, boy is used to describe all males below the age of 18 and 'men' is used to describe all males over the age of 18.

'Boy' may be used by males as an accepted part of their intra-group communication strategies to confirm membership of a core group. However, such terminology would not generally be accepted when used by others who are not group members, for example tutors of teachers.

Black

Before providing the definition of Black used in this inquiry, I briefly explore the concept of race, because race is intrinsically linked to notions of identity and ethnicity. Gillborn offers the following observation

> 'Race' is a word we all recognise. Part of the English language for hundreds of years, the term has been the subject of heated political debate for more than a century. And yet for all the controversy, it is still the case that people routinely (often unthinkingly) categorise themselves and others according to 'racial' criteria. (1995:1)

Like the concept itself, ideas regarding race are fluid and subject to changing fashions and opinions. Initially race was viewed as a fixed biological feature with various immutable, inherited characteristics such as intelligence and physical ability which were ascribed to different groups according to their race. Although 'arguments about fixed genetic differences and the innate superiority of certain human 'races' have been widely discredited' (*ibid*:3), such ideas are capable of 'still capturing the popular imagination' (Mirza, 2009:43) and continue to exert an influence on 'our thinking about race' (*ibid*). Rather than being fixed by genetics, race is now considered to be 'a system of socially constructed and enforced categories, constantly recreated and modified through human interaction' (Gillborn, 1995:3).

While there may be no scientific basis for race, the impact of the 'physical, phenotypical, external, visible difference' (Mirza, 2009:43) continues to be experienced, felt and lived by Black people in Britain today. As recently as 2007, James Watson who, together with Francis Crick, famously unravelled the DNA double helix, reignited the race debate in an interview for the *Sunday Times*, where he 'translated the careful wording of his book into language of the street. People expect everyone to be equal, he claimed, but 'people who have to deal with Black employees find this not so' (Malik, 2008:2), suggesting there is a potential inferiority or some difficulty that characterises Black people.

For my research it was important to establish a clear definition of who could be considered Black and therefore eligible to participate in this research. A definition was needed which acknowledged the 'enduring nature (of visible recognition) as a source of stigma' (Mendoza-Denton and Downey, 2002:898), allowed for self-classification and accommodated the politicisation of being Black in Britain. For this research, being described as Black meant more than simple historical or geographical attachment and had three principal features:

▦   Firstly, would most other people identify them as a Black person?

- Secondly, did they consider and believe themselves to be Black?
- And finally, as well as personally identifying themselves as Black, did they identify with and align themselves to this group?

This three-fold definition was used because it accommodated issues of visibility, identity construction and individual personal alignment. Although Black does not describe a nation state or a geographical location, it is used as a way of naming and describing a group of people with a collective identity. For this reason Black is used with a capital letter throughout this book, in the same way as would be required when referring to English, Indian, Canadian or any other group of people with a shared cultural identity.

White

In the same way that Black is used to describe a group of people who share a common historical and geographical heritage, White is used to describe all people who appear to be visibly White. In common with the notion of Black people, the notion of White also crosses national and geographical boundaries. Within the context of this research, it is also linked to those who have traditionally held authority, power and decision making capabilities.

Secondary education

I use the term 'secondary education' to describe education from the ages of 11 to 16, as this encompasses compulsory secondary schooling within the UK. Although all students in the UK are now obliged to continue in education or employment with training until the age of 18 I have not considered other environments outside the school system.

FE

FE means general further education colleges (GFECs) that offer a broad range of both academic and vocational education packages to students over the age of 16 and link provision for students aged 14-16. It is important not to confuse FE with the more generic Adult Education sector. Adult Education is an umbrella term used to describe other adult education and training and includes various government funded organisations, voluntary organisations, work based, charitable and religious groups providing leisure, academic, recreational and vocational provision (Kelly, 1992; Rowntree and Binns, 1985). The concern of my study was far more tightly defined and only considered publicly funded colleges that provided education, training and leisure opportunities for students over the age of 16.

The research environment

Both of the FE colleges used in this inquiry are located in a large conurbation in the Midlands: one urban with an ethnically mixed and diverse client group, and the other suburban with a largely White client group. Employment in the area had changed over time, as the traditional industries of production and manufacturing had declined, to be replaced by newer leisure and retail industries, as the principal employers of the region. The urban college is located in a relatively prosperous area, with high levels of employment and owner-occupied homes. The other is on the outskirts of the city in a slightly less affluent suburban area, although still with good rates of employment and high levels of home ownership. Both colleges are in largely White neighbourhoods. The urban college attracted an ethnically mixed population and many ethnic minority students attended, whereas the suburban college attracted students principally from its immediate White neighbourhood.

Both colleges were medium sized general further education colleges (GFECs), each attended by approximately 20,000 students on multiple sites. Each provided a range of further, higher and vocational education courses for learners aged 14 upwards, as well as a choice of leisure and recreation programmes. In addition to the full and part-time courses available during the day, evening and at weekends, both colleges provided opportunities for flexi-, distance and on-line learning. All the Black men and boys who engaged with this inquiry completed their studies on a single college site. Neither college nor their campuses had a reputation for violence or disruption, although both employed security staff who maintained a visible profile and learners often had their identity checked when they entered college premises.

Both colleges prided themselves on the extensive range of courses they offered, the quality of teaching and the high level of student support offered to students. This support included personal tutor support, professional development coaching, welfare advice and personal counselling. The colleges also had extensive support mechanisms for students with additional learning needs. However, despite a growing population of Black and ethnic minority students neither college had considered providing specified support for this group.

The research participants

I invited students who were studying at different levels and on different programmes to participate in the research. All 29 students who engaged with the study identified themselves as Black according to the definition given earlier. However, a formal national census would have described many of the participants as mixed race, as they had one Black and one White parent. The participants ranged in age from 16 to 47, although all but three were under 25, and only the three older learners lived independently in their own accommodation. All the others lived at home in a family unit. For most of the participants family comprised a single parent, generally the mother, and other siblings. All participants except the three older students received the Educational Maintenance Allowance (EMA).

Before they came to college the participants had attended various establishments. Seven of the participants attended college the previous year on a lower level programme and two had been in full-time employment. One had been on a supported education programme co-ordinated by a day centre and had ongoing mental health concerns. The remaining 19 had transferred straight from secondary school. One of these reported he had attended two different secondary schools as a consequence of permanent exclusions. Another who had been permanently excluded from his second secondary school, had been placed on an 'education otherwise' programme, whereby he was allowed to attend college on a full-time basis. Four other participants had been given fixed term exclusions, but had been allowed to return to their school.

The learners who took part in the inquiry were studying a variety of options, including an individualised learning programme, sports, computing, art, business and music technology courses, at a range of levels from entry through to advanced level. While they were completing their studies at college, 17 of the group held down part-time jobs working in shops, restaurants or leisure centres. Although some were employed in an area of personal interest related to their chosen career, most worked solely for the extra source of income. All had ambitions to continue their studies beyond their current course to complete another programme at college or progress onto higher education.

Methodology

My research sought to explore the lived experiences and daily realities of Black men and boys in the post-compulsory sector. While there are various reports concerning the educational experience of Black boys in schools and others about the experience of Black men in higher education, there is a dearth of information on what happens to this group once they enter FE. In order to investigate the research question it was critical to use an approach capable of capturing the feelings and emotions of the Black men and boys who took part in my inquiry so I could provide a personalised, situated account of their experience. For this reason an 'interpretivisit, qualitative style of research' (Henn, Weinstein and Foard, 2006:18) was chosen, supplemented by additional data relating to their academic achievement. The research suited an interpretivisit approach also because my purpose was 'not to explain why something happens, but to explore [and] build up an understanding of something we have little or no knowledge of' (*ibid*:15). Interpretivism enabled me to work with the Black students to 'provide an account of their world in their own words' (*ibid*:14) and so to illuminate the under researched area.

To investigate the research question I used multiple complementary techniques to collect data and capture the experiences of the research participants. These included focus groups, individual interviews, observations, photo-records and course achievement data. Such a wide range of techniques was needed because each technique revealed new information and so built up a composite, detailed understanding of the Black men and boys' experience of their lives while studying in college.

Focus groups

Focus groups were the principal method of data generation, chosen because they provided a mechanism for the Black men and boys to speak openly and freely, supported by their peers. This approach also allowed the students to develop a collective understanding of different aspects of FE. Focus groups generate 'vivid and rich descriptions' (American Statistical Association, 1997: 1) from 'a small number of carefully selected people' (*ibid*) and were suited to the open-ended exploratory nature of this research. I favoured this technique also because it provided an opportunity for the participants 'to be valued as experts' (Gibbs, 1997:3) which, since they were a marginalised and sometimes excluded group, was a key reason for adopting this technique. Bringing the students together in small groups allowed them to take control of the discussions and to direct the agenda.

However, because 'focus groups favour extraverts' (Coventry University, online) who are skilled in spontaneously expressing their views, focus groups may be unsuitable for participants who, although not lacking in things to say, may have difficulties in expressing their views. To overcome this dilemma, prompt cards identifying specific topics regarding FE were provided (see appendix 2). To avoid the danger of leading the group, suggestions were drawn from previous research narratives relating the educational experience of Black men and boys and were therefore phrased in accessible student language.

While prompt cards could arguably pre-determine the scope of the discussion, this is unlikely as 'by its very nature, focus group research is open ended and cannot be entirely predetermined (Gibbs, 1997:3). The prompt card format provided further support to the participants by giving them tangible artefacts to hold and focus their attentions accordingly.

Individual interviews

Information collected from focus groups was complemented by additional data collected through individual interviews and used to conduct a more detailed examination of issues which had surfaced during focus group sessions.

'Power relations which structure interview settings are never more obvious than when the biographies of the interviewer and the interviewee(s) are inscribed in different social practices and discourses' (Scott and Usher, 1999: 114). Other researchers state this 'issue may be exacerbated ... when we study groups with whom we do not share membership' (Miller and Glassner, 1998: 101). However, I shared a common heritage with the Black men and boys who took part in this inquiry, so the individual interviews were appropriate and worthwhile. They had even greater value as they allowed...

> interviewees to talk about the subject in terms of their own frame of reference. In doing so, the method enables the interviewer to maximise her or his understanding of the respondent's point of view. (Henn, Weinstein and Foard, 2006: 161)

This frame of reference was an important aspect of the data collection, for although the focus group had the advantage of acting in a mutually supportive way for the participants, it was not possible to tell how much of the information shared was designed to impress either me or their peers. I was aware that weaker data is sometimes produced when the 'respondent is in the presence of others, in group settings' (Miles and Huberman, 1994:268). Using individual interviews removed any potential peer pressure and provided an opportunity for students to make statements without the need to impress a wider audience.

I used an informal, semi-structured format so that 'to all intents and purposes (the interview was) like a normal conversation' (Bartlett and Burton, 2007:43). Such an approach provided opportunities for in-depth exploration of issues where questions could be 'fully expanded at the discretion of the interviewer and the interviewee, and can be enhanced by probes' (Schensul, Schensul and LeCompte, 1999:149). A skeleton framework of ten questions was used as a guide for the individual interviews so there would be consistency across the sample group, and although the further probing questions were individual, all participants were asked the same common core of questions (see appendix 1). All interviews were tape recorded and later transcribed.

Observations

Further data was collected through observations carried out in both academic and social settings in the urban college. Observations were conducted at a distance to minimise the likelihood of students feeling they were under surveillance and their consent was obtained in advance. Observations were naturalistic in that 'the situation being observed [was] not contrived for research purposes' (Punch, 2005:179) and served as a way of obtaining a 'more valid and holistic picture of society than that which could be acquired by remaining true to only one set of methods' (Henn, Weinstein and Foard, 2006:19).

To allow the Black men and boys to become familiar with any new tutors they might have, classroom observations began five months into the inquiry so the students had time to become orientated to their surroundings and staff. Social space observations started at the beginning of the inquiry and were completed on an informal and ad hoc basis. My access to observation venues was facilitated by the ease with which I was 'accepted into the situation' (*ibid*:93) thanks to my position as a staff member and the common features I shared with the Black students in terms of 'language, class background, manner ... race and ethnicity' (*ibid*:93).

Photo-records

Photographs were used to enable the Black men and boys to provide 'expert testimony about their experiences, associations and lifestyles' (Thomson, 2008:1). Selected students were given disposable 'point and shoot cameras' (Mitchell, 2011:51) and instructed to use the cameras to record images of what life in FE meant to them and which they believed symbolised their lives in FE. By asking students to select images which represented their experiences of college life, I was able to access new information and to explore 'rich (and mostly untapped) possibilities' (*ibid*, 2011:36) of the realities of life in FE.

The students were able to take as many or as few pictures as they wished and could request a second camera if they chose. Because this data was not collected by experienced researchers the selected pictures may have lacked refinement. However, the images presented a different and further means of gaining deeper understanding of the Black men and boys' experience, and a mechanism for surfacing ideas and themes that it might have been taboo for them to discuss in an open forum.

Because 'an image can be read in multiple ways' (Thomson, 2008:10), all the participants had an individual debriefing meeting where they discussed and explained but did not have to justify the pictures they had taken, spelling out the importance of each of their selected images. This was particularly important as, according to Thomson, images taken by young people 'may not be amenable to straightforward adult meanings'.

Numerical data

I obtained Learning and Skills Council (LSC) data on the academic achievement of students categorised by ethnicity and by age bracket for the urban college. Unfortunately, although this data showed achievement according to ethnicity, it was not disaggregated by gender, and Black males and Black females were listed together. But the data was still useful as it showed the group's overall achievement in a college wide context and in relation to their White peers.

Structure of the book

The book is divided into four parts. It begins by identifying and framing the issues, and ends with suggesting strategies for change. It is written within the context of FE and each chapter relates to a key issue regarding the education of Black men and boys in the post-compulsory sector. It is therefore of particular interest to anyone who teaches Black men and boys and works in FE. However, the appeal and application of this book is much wider than FE. It is relevant to anyone who has taught, is teaching or who may at some time teach Black men and boys in higher, further, secondary or primary education. It is for all educators who believe in social justice and are committed to supporting Black men and boys to achieve their academic potential. The book gives voice to the concerns of Black men and boys in their own words and points to significant factors which would enhance their experience of education in the future.

Part one provides a contextual overview for the study and describes the academic location of Black boys at secondary school level. The data available on school provision is then compared to their academic achievement in FE. To provide a wider picture of their educational experience, the social positioning of Black men and boys in both secondary education and FE is also considered. In part two, the structural organisation and culture of FE colleges is directly compared with the organisation and culture of secondary schools. Black youths discuss how the organisation of the curriculum influenced their motivation to study and the impact of different institutional cultures on their learning and achievement.

In part three, possible choices available to Black boys and men regarding learning are considered. Chapter 5 describes the impact of race on student choice at different stages of their education from 'humbled emasculated conformity' to 'destructive rebel' (Sewell, 1997:xvii) and how in turn such choices influence students' achievement. The role and range of support systems and the way in which different types of support interact to promote academic achievement is reviewed in Chapter 6. Other more problematic support mechanisms are also considered in this chapter. Chapter 7 details the ways in which Black boys and men have worked to establish their own support systems which operate independently of mainstream college support mechanisms and shows how these home grown systems have enabled them to persist and succeed within FE.

Part four looks forward to the future and, optimistically and ambitiously, identifies an agenda for change for FE to support Black men and boys. What actions are feasible? What would be the training implications for tutors and managers? Are Black students left with no option other than to become a destructive stereotype of Black masculinity, or can colleges and schools work differently to encourage Black men and boys to engage positively with their education? The final chapter ends on a cautionary note and looks realistically at the challenges of implementing systems to promote change.

Recognising, accepting and believing that research is not only influenced by the topic and the environment in which it takes place, but also and critically by those who have carried out the research (Kincheloe, 1991; Griffiths, 1998) I would like the reader to know that I am a Black woman, the child of a Black Jamaican Windrush traveller father and a White English mother. Although social class is not determined by socio-economic location at birth, I certainly grew up in a working class family and attended state schools throughout my compulsory schooling. All this was significant in the way I completed the investigation and the relationship I developed with the Black students who took part in my study. Paradoxically, while my race served to bring me closer to the research group and facilitated the research process, the other defining feature of my identity, my gender, served to distance and set me apart from them. However, I believe my race and gender combined synergetically and acted 'as an aid rather than an impediment' (Ram, 1996:124) to the research. Almost like an older aunt, I was sufficiently connected to understand the daily lives of the Black men and boys, while at the same time, I maintained sufficient critical distance to see their worlds objectively.

2

Black men and boys' academic and social location in education: a contextual overview

Introduction

Before considering the academic and social location of Black men and boys in the FE sector, we need to be aware of their overall positioning within secondary schooling. Over time, Black boys have come to occupy an unenviable position within education, being variously portrayed as aggressive underachievers with attitude problems and limited academic ability, as sexual predators more intent on progressing their next conquest than doing well at school or as small-time weapon carrying gangsters trying to seal assorted illegal deals. Such presentations are not readily compatible with high academic achievement or social inclusion. As recently as 2011 Adolph Cameron, head of the Jamaica Teachers' Association, speaking at an event organised by the National Union of Teachers (NUT) said Black 'boys are more interested in hustling, which is a quick way of making money, rather than making the commitment to study' (BBC News, 2011, online), thus affirming the existing preconceptions of some teachers.

The historic and contemporary picture of Black boys in mainstream UK education requires detailed explanation, for it is against this background that Black boys in schools and Black men in FE continue to be judged and it is within this context that intervention strategies to promote success are assessed. Research suggests that many African-Caribbean students routinely fail academically in the UK secondary education sector, while socially they are marginalised, isolated and excluded (Nehusi and Gosling, 2001; Gillborn, 2008). This representation suggests that the responsibility for failure lies

17

solely with African-Caribbean boys themselves. An alternative explanation for this situation is, however, that these students are failed by an unresponsive, hostile system which has little idea of and even less interest in how to cater effectively for their needs. The purpose of this chapter is to review the academic and social position of Black boys within compulsory secondary education and to compare this with their academic positioning in the FE sector.

The academic location of black boys in secondary education

The underachievement of and the discrimination against Black students, and in particular the underachievement of Black boys, has been well documented for secondary education in the UK. As early as 1971 Hackney teacher Bernard Coard, is his seminal book: *How the West Indian Child is Made Educationally Sub-Normal in the British School System*, drew attention to the inappropriate and inaccurate assessment of Black students and their disproportionate placement in Special Educational Needs (SEN) schools and lower sets and streams. For its time, Coard's report was groundbreaking. It challenged the education system itself, identifying the structures and processes of the system and revealing how these, coupled with the prevailing attitudes of teaching staff, caused Black students to be ill served and to underachieve. Coard presented the underachievement of Black students as a problem for the whole Black community in Britain, not just the individuals or families concerned. He stressed the educational, moral and social responsibility of mainstream schools, the government and education authorities to recognise and confront these issues and provide a just system of education for all Black children.

However, it was not until the 1980s that mainstream education finally caught up with Black community opinion and fully embraced the concerns identified by Coard, first in the 1981 Rampton Report and later with the 1985 Swann Report. Both Rampton and Swann unequivocally confirmed Coard's earlier findings and showed West Indian students, as they were called then, to be academically underperforming in comparison to *all* their peers. Data collected by the Department for Education and Science (DES) for the Swann Report showed there were serious issues regarding the number of 'West Indians, Asians and other leavers obtaining five or more higher grades (grades A-C at 'O' level or CSE grade 1) and only 6 per cent of West Indian leavers in 1981/82 had obtained this level of qualification' (Swann, 1985:114). This low level of attainment represented an achievement gap of over 60 per cent between West Indian and other students.

O levels and CSEs were replaced in 1988 by the General Certificate of Secondary Education (GCSE). Now all students were effectively entered for the same examination and all were assessed on the same scale. While this addressed a previous inequality of Black students being disproportionately allocated to less prestigious CSE classes, the benchmark recognised as a good pass remained at obtaining a grade C or above. The following table, taken from Gillborn's and Mizra's analysis of student achievement from 1988 to 1997, demonstrates that while there were improvements in the achievement rates of Black students during this time, they still lagged behind all other ethnic minority groups, except Pakistani students. By1997 Black and Pakistani students were showing identical achievement levels, indicating the rate of improvement for Black students was lower than that of other ethnic groups.

Ethnic Group	Percentage of Students Gaining Five or More Higher Grade Passes			Percentage Improvement from 1988-1997
	1988	1995	1997	
White	26	42	44	18
Black	17	21	28	11
Indian	23	44	49	26
Pakistani	20	22	28	8
Bangladeshi	13	23	32	19

Table 1: Comparison by Ethnicity of GCSE Attainment for England and Wales in 1988, 1995, 1997 (State Schools Only)
Source: Adapted from Gillborn and Mizra, 2003:13

The continuing underachievement of Black students relative to their peers prompted Ofsted to observe that 'at secondary level, the data indicates that Black Caribbean pupils underachieve. In some cases they are the lowest performing group at GCSE level' (1999:11). Other research data mirrored this position of constant underachievement and an independent study completed by the London Development Agency showed

> for 2000, 2001 and 2002 ... African-Caribbean boys have consistently been the lowest performing group across all key stages. The achievement gap widened with progress through each key stage. Even where there was year on year progress, the performance of African-Caribbean boys remained significantly below that of other groups. (2004:9)

Although as the next table shows there were significant improvements in the percentage of Black pupils gaining five or more good GCSEs between 2003 and 2005, they still remained the lowest achieving group during this time. Further, any gains made decrease in significance because overall 'attainment rates at GCSE (rose) in general' (Bhattacharyya *et al*, 2003:10). Unfortunately for Black students, this advancement has not been sustained with time and Black students remain among the lowest achieving groups of all students.

Ethnic Group	Gender	Percentage National Average of Students Gaining 5 or More Higher Grades			
		2002-03%	2003-04%	2004-05%	Percentage Change 2003-2005
Black African	Boys	34.1	45.5	42.9	8.8
	Girls	46.8	61.2	53.3	6.5
Black Caribbean	Boys	25.1	27.6	33.3	8.2
	Girls	40.3	43.8	49.4	9.1
Black Other	Boys	27.2	29.0	33.7	6.5
	Girls	40.3	42.3	50.8	10.5
White/Black Caribbean	Boys	39.5	44.9	48.4	8.9
	Girls	55.1	53.6	62.1	7.0
Indian	Boys	60.3	63.3	64.8	4.5
	Girls	70.3	77.1	75.8	5.5
White	Boys	46.2	47.5	50.3	4.1
	Girls	56.7	57.5	60.2	3.5

Table 2: Percentage of Students Achieving 5 or More Higher Grade GCSEs by Ethnic Group and Gender (2003 to 2005)
Source: Tikly et al, 2006:Table 16

Other research completed at a similar time indicated that...

> while attainment continue(d) to rise for White, Pakistani and Bangladeshi pupils in 2002, it fell back for Black pupils ... In 2002 approximately a third of Black pupils achieved five or more A*-C GCSEs compared to half of White pupils. In addition, of those Black pupils who achieved 5 or more GCSEs A*-C, about half achieved very high results (8 or more A*-C) compared to two-thirds of all other ethnic groups. (Bhattacharyya *et al*, 2003:10)

More recent statistical evidence from the Department for Children, Schools and Families (DCSF) on Key Stage 4 attainment for 2008-09 has echoed this pattern and showed that 'the lowest achieving group were Black Caribbean, Pakistani, Other Black and pupils from a Mixed White and Black Caribbean background' (DCSF, 2010, online), thus replicating previous findings with Black boys remaining stubbornly anchored at the very lowest end of achievement.

Despite significant changes to the school curriculum, including the introduction of GCSEs and the National Curriculum, the problem of Black student underachievement has neither diminished nor disappeared since Coard first identified this matter in 1971. Central government changes to education have had little impact on the overall achievement rates of African-Caribbean students. Other ethnic groups, with the exception of Traveller students, have not been subject to the same level of disadvantage. Damningly, the problem of underachievement for African-Caribbean boys becomes even more exaggerated as they progress through secondary school so that after making 'a sound start in primary schools their performance shows a marked decline at secondary level' (Ofsted, 1999:7). This problem is exacerbated by a 'worrying ignorance generally, about how to raise the attainment of Black Caribbean boys' (*ibid*:8). Consequently, Black pupils find themselves in educational double jeopardy where they are not supported to attain qualifications at the required level and where schools appear to lack the necessary skills, knowledge, understanding and possibly even the will, to support them in achieving such qualifications.

Although the majority of available evidence points to the underachievement and marginalisation of Black students in schools, some schools are helping Black students to achieve academic success. In *Achievement of Black Caribbean Pupils: Good Practice in Secondary Schools*, Ofsted worked with six comprehensive schools and identified common features that helped Black Caribbean students to succeed. These schools provided high levels of student support, had explicit expectations of all students, a productive work-focused ethos and clear and unambiguous leadership which encouraged all pupils to achieve good examination results (Ofsted, 2002). When compared to similar schools, these schools challenged national trends and produced higher levels of attainment for their Black Caribbean pupils.

Other government initiatives such as *Aim Higher* have also helped schools to improve the academic attainment of African and Caribbean pupils. However, while individual pupils in selected schools may have benefited from this intervention strategy, the initiative was not rolled out nationwide and the academic achievement of Black males remains below that of most of their peer group overall (Tikly *et al*, 2006).

The academic location of black boys and men in FE

In spite of having an academically unproductive time while at school, many Black students, are positively motivated to continue their education in FE and to 'persevere with their education in the hope of improving their prospects and obtaining their desired occupation' (Fyfe and Figueroa, 1993:234). This positive motivation to remain in education could be a direct result of under-achieving at school and, in common with others who have not attained their goals, they view FE as opportunity to gain 'what they feel they have missed and what they believe carries most status: academic qualifications' (FEU, 1985:5). This strong positive motivation and pro-educational stance was also evidenced by Eggleston, who found a 'persistence and determination of Afro-Caribbean young people to pursue qualifications through further education' (1986:30). Eggleston's research originates from the latter half of the twentieth century, yet this situation persists. Recent research from the National Institute of Adult Continuing Education, England and Wales (NIACE), found that 'Africans (82%), people of mixed ethnic origin (80%), other minority ethnic groups (79%) and Caribbeans (72%) exhibit higher than average levels of participation in learning' (Aldridge and Tuckett, 2003:7) in the FE. Bhatta-charyya *et al* also found that despite being 'alienated by previous experiences of schooling' (2003:24) Black students wished to continue their education and saw college as a 'chance to re-enter education and mainstream opportunities' (*ibid*).

With such strong positive motivation to remain in education it would be morally derelict for students to continue to FE only to have their school ex-periences replicated in the tertiary sector. Many FE colleges appear to be aware of this situation and the findings in *Race Equality in Further Education: A Report by HMI*, indicate

> learners from all ethnic backgrounds are increasingly succeeding in achieving their qualifications in the FE sector. Overall success rates for learners of BME heritage of all ages increased at an above average rate between 2002 and 2004. For 16-18 year old learners, particularly in GFE colleges, there were some significant improvements for particular groups whose success rates were excep-tionally low previously, such as Bangladeshi, Black Caribbean and Black Other learners. (Ofsted, 2005:16)

Evidence is limited at this stage and the Ofsted survey did not claim to be a nationwide survey of all FE colleges or representative of the entire FE sector. However, 41 colleges participated in the survey, which represented approxi-mately 10 per cent of FE colleges nationally. More significantly, a critical finding of this survey was that, whereas schools do not appear to be supporting or promoting achievement of their Black pupils, FE colleges are achieving some degree of success in doing so. The report shows that, in contrast to schools where Black students are underachieving at all levels, their success in FE 'increased at an above average rate' (*ibid*:16) for three consecutive years. In comparison to the maintained sector, it appears that Black students in FE are being given the opportunity to participate and to achieve.

The social positioning of black boys in secondary schools

The social position occupied by Black boys and men within education is the consequence of a number of distinct, yet interconnected entities. Firstly there are the Black students themselves, who have a racialised and gendered collective understanding of what it means to be a Black male in society (Majors and Billson, 1992; Noguera, 2003); secondly there are the academic and other staff who formulate views of this group and occupy a powerful site from which they influence how Black students are accommodated by the organisation (Verma and Bagley, 1983; White-Hood, 1994; Wright *et al*, 1998); and thirdly there is the corporate body which use staff and other mechanisms to locate Black learners within the structure as a whole (Sewell, 1997; Solorzano *et al*, 2000; Blair, 2001). The collective interaction of these different units act to produce a social positioning of Black males which is both gendered and racialised.

In secondary education Black boys occupy a unique position. Their maleness has created a 'perceived physical threat of African Caribbean boys [which is] located within stereotypical notions of Black masculinity' (Sewell, 1997:40). Simultaneously their race, even though many students were born in the UK, has positioned them as outsiders to the dominant White culture. The combination of these factors means the identity of Black boys in schools is a production of both their personal construction and the ruling hegemony which has previously portrayed them as 'one big lump of rebellious, phallocentric underachievers' (Sewell, 2004:103).

Consequently, Black students have frequently reported being subjected to open and subtle discrimination, inadequate or hostile teacher attention and disproportionably high levels of exclusion (Mac an Ghaill 1988; London Development Agency, 2004) during their time in schools. Sewell's (1997) account in particular describes how Black boys have been portrayed as sexually intimidating and violent, resulting in both formal and informal exclusions. Further attempts by students to be actively engaged in their learning have been misinterpreted by teachers as aggression and 'for some, simply attempting to express an opinion was perceived as being rude and a challenge to the teacher's authority' (London Development Agency, 2004:8).

In her work Blair found that for many Black students schooling which 'was difficult enough' (2001:73) in the primary sector had become an almost impossible 'obstacle course' by the time they reached secondary school. They were routinely 'represented as violent, aggressive, sexually out of control and engaged in illicit activities such as mugging and drug pushing' (*ibid*: 81), excluded from actively participating in their own education and socially marginalised. As a response to this situation, Black students have created alternative sub-cultures and spaces as a means of survival. But when Black students congregated in corridors during break times as a means of creating their own social spaces, they 'frequently attracted the attention of the teacher or teachers on break duty (and) the teacher often responded to this situation by interrogatively ushering the group out of the corridor' (Wright *et al*, 1998:76) suggesting school staff seemed to believe the only reason for Black pupils meeting together was to engage in some kind of wrongdoing. Similarly, research by the London Development Agency found that Black students were often 'wrongly accused, watched with suspicion at lunchtimes, subject to negative stereotyping and simply being disliked on account of being Black' (2004:8).

These hostile teacher perceptions were replicated in other locations and when in the classroom Black students received negative tutor attention or were excluded from academic conversations. Exchanges between Black students and teachers were usually characterised by their being 'overlooked for answering questions, verbal aggression from teachers, and harsher reprimands than for students from other ethnic backgrounds for the same misdemeanour' (London Development Agency, 2004:7). Black students were aware of such staff attitudes and reported that they were not 'listened to or understood by White teachers' (*ibid*:8).

Conclusion

This chapter has traced a consistent picture from the 1980s onwards of academic underachievement of Black male students, who have achieved considerably lower levels of attainment than their peers of all races. More recent data from 2008-09 from the DCSF has only confirmed earlier statistics regarding the educational achievement of Black children in British schools, with African-Caribbean children showing one of the lowest levels of attainment, and operating on the very fringes of educational achievement.

However, this bleak picture has not been replicated in FE. During their time in FE, unlike in schools, Black boys and men have been supported to engage with education in a way that was denied in mainstream secondary schools. As a result of this increased engagement, Black boys have been able to recover some educational ground lost during secondary school when they get to FE and the achievement levels for Black students in general in FE have exceeded their attainment rates at secondary schooling.

PART TWO
FE CULTURE AND ORGANISATIONS

3

The institutional culture of FE colleges

Introduction

Institutional culture is important because it is felt and experienced by everyone who attends an organisation. Everyone who attends college has their own personalised understanding of institutional culture, but there is no agreed definition of the primary purpose of colleges. Defining college culture is further complicated by the historical lack of direction from central government, and the colleges' obligation to be responsive to the changing needs of the local community and business. These competing influences have produced different pressures on FE, and college culture has evolved into 'a rich tapestry woven and modified over the years to meet the changing needs of industry, commerce, the public sector and students' (Hall, 1994:42) as colleges have tried to marry the diverse impacts of market forces and student choice.

Cultures develop partly a result of the formal rules and regulations which inform the day to day practices of an organisation, partly because of historical legacies which have become accepted as the agreed norms of an institution and, crucially, partly as a result of the way college policies and procedures are interpreted and implemented by staff. In colleges institutional culture has become shorthand for the understood code by which colleges operate and the behaviour college members are expected demonstrate. In everyday language, institutional culture simply describes the *feel* of the place. And while 'people will forget what you've said, people will forget what you did, people will never forget how you made them feel' (Angelou, cited in Kelly, 2003:310). Black people have had many different experiences of education and these have informed how they feel about the UK education system. Members of the Black community continue to carry these memories and feelings with them.

In this chapter I describe how the institutional culture of colleges has impacted on Black men and boys to shape their experiences of colleges and their feelings towards the FE sector. I clarify where colleges are located in relation to secondary and higher education and explain how the historical origins of colleges have helped to produce the unique culture of the sector.

The location of FE in relation to secondary schools and higher education

It is easy to provide a simplistic definition of the structural location of the FE sector, as 'somewhere between the compulsory school sector and industry and higher education' (Frankel and Reeves, 1996:6). This perception of the sector still exists to a degree, but such a basic description hides the real complexity of the sector and certainly gives no indication of the ongoing turbulence and changes experienced by FE in recent years. Now more than ever, describing where FE fits relative to secondary and higher education (HE) has become a difficult and challenging task which has been made more difficult by the government's ongoing determination that much more undergraduate provision, such as foundation degrees, should be and need to be delivered by FE colleges.

Since the 1990s FE colleges have been encouraged to expand and have been a key part of successive government strategies for 'achieving higher levels of skills and qualifications' (Lucas, 2004:29) across the nation. Part of this expansion has been the introduction of the Increased Flexibility Programme (IFP) and the HE in FE initiative.

The IFP was introduced into schools and colleges in 2002 to provide 'vocational learning for 14 to 16 year olds' (Ofsted, 2005:1) who would benefit from being in a different learning environment. To achieve this, secondary schools entered into partnerships with FE colleges and work-based learning providers to provide a 'more diverse curriculum' (*ibid*:2) and vocational learning opportunities for some young people. Under this provision young people attended FE colleges or other providers for part of their week to study 'National Vocational Qualifications (NVQs) or other vocational qualifications' (*ibid*) while still enrolled at school, such as hair and beauty, care, motor vehicle maintenance and construction. Pupils who participated in this provision have positively benefited from the experience and 'overall, students in the IFP cohort gained more points than might have been expected given their prior attainment and other background characteristics' (Golden *et al*, 2005: 35). The IFP programme has been so successful that it has expanded each year since its introduction and many more 14-16 year olds are now engaging in FE programmes. This expansion is expected to continue, so more young people will complete part of their education in a college environment than ever before.

Similarly, the government has adopted one of Dearing's key recommendations in his 1997 Report to widen participation in HE by introducing two-year work-focused foundation degrees. Consistent with the government's aim to deliver more undergraduate programmes through FE, there has been an unprecedented expansion of the number of students studying HE-level courses in colleges. FE has responded to these new demands positively and has developed new vocational programmes and other HE level courses. In 2003 there were 162 colleges providing such diverse courses as medicine, linguistics and performing arts at HNC/D, foundation degree, diploma, BA and MSc level, targeted at learners who wanted an HE experience, but for whom traditional university attendance was unsuitable.

FE has continued to grow and evolve to meet changing demands, despite having a relatively 'low profile on the national stage' (Foster, 2005:8). The simplistic portrayal of FE as being the 'bit in the middle', as quoted earlier, no longer applies and the following account provided by Lucas provides a more accurate description of the simultaneously invisible but significant FE sector, which can best be described as

> caught half-way between full-time students and part-time students. Furthermore they [colleges] offer vocational and academic courses and provide programmes such as HNDs, as well as those geared to adults needing basic skills and those wishing to gain access to higher education. In other words FE colleges can be seen as both preparatory and lifelong learning institutions, as institutions contributing to national training targets, and as organisations responsive to local needs. It is this legacy of diversity and lack of a clear strategic mission that distinguishes the FE sector so clearly from schools and universities. (2004:39)

The historical origins of FE and the impact on college culture

Hall states that 'most further education colleges have grown from either the former Mechanics' Institutes or technical schools' (1994:2). Mechanics' Institutes were independent organisations which had two principal objectives: to provide technical education to working men, in the belief that a better educated adult workforce would be more efficient and effective in performing their working duties and, secondly, to promote appropriate social attitudes among the working population (Hall, 1994; Green and Lucas, 2000). As voluntary non-governmental organisations, Mechanics' Institutes were obliged to obtain their own funding and received support from industrialists who wanted a skilled workforce and from prominent philanthropists who believed that education would help to counter the twin sins of 'immorality and alcoholism' (Fieldhouse, 1998:27) thought to be prevalent among the working classes, and who were concerned to provide working men with an alternative to gambling and spending their time and money in public houses,.

Although they were not polar opposites, there was a dichotomous tension between these two funding sources: the motivation for industrialists was directly linked to the needs of commerce, while the philanthropists were driven by an ethical agenda to improve the moral character of the workforce. Thus two diverse viewpoints were brought together in one establishment: the idea of principled self-improvement advocated by well meaning philanthropists and the skill-based needs of industry promoted by business.

The 1944 Education Act established the system of education that we still recognise today, when education was organised 'into three progressive stages: primary, secondary and further education' (Fieldhouse, 1998:58) and local authorities were required to 'provide secondary education for all their children over eleven' (Rubenstein and Simon, 1973:35). The Act, described FE as all 'full-time and part-time education for persons over compulsory school age' which provided 'full and part-time general education and vocational training as well as (non-vocational) social and recreational education provision' (Frankel and Reeves, 1996:7).

Before the FE sector was established, students exited school either directly into work or, for a privileged few, continued into higher education. FE colleges, originally included in the unregulated Adult Education sector, were a response to a growing demand for education beyond compulsory schooling intended to serve the needs of both the wider community and commerce (Kelly, 1992; Fieldhouse, 1998). These two key factors have helped to create the culture of colleges. While the 1944 Education Act established an age related, staged education system, compulsory education only applied to the primary and secondary sectors. The Act also introduced technical secondary schools which provided practical specialist vocational education designed to facilitate young people's entry into work.

In contrast to secondary education, FE remains an elective educational opportunity which individuals opt into deliberately. The voluntary nature of FE was embedded in the 1944 Education Act, which did not 'insist that LEAs provide, only that they secure, adequate provision' (Fieldhouse, 1998:103) for the post-16 population, emphasising the lower priority accorded to FE. It was not until 1992 when the Further and Higher Education Act 'created a newly defined further education sector' (*ibid*:75) that FE gained a higher profile in government. Clarification of the purpose of FE was provided in the 2005 14-19 Education and Skills White Paper, which declared a government ambition to 'encourage a culture of staying on and achieving worthwhile qualifications until 19' (DfES, 2005:82). However, FE was one of many providers who could support this goal. As a consequence of this difference, optional and choice driven as opposed to compulsory, FE has always been customer orientated, providing subjects and courses to meet demand. This fundamental difference has helped to create the significant cultural differences that exist between secondary schools and FE.

From its beginnings FE has been non-compulsory responding to the needs of the market. In many ways FE, like the early Mechanics' Institutes before them, still retains a somewhat schizophrenic personality, split between different agendas, attempting to meet the needs of industry, employers and the community in an uneasy and sometimes difficult balance. Echoes of its elective participation, the self-help ethos and close links with industry can be traced back to its roots in the Mechanics' Institutes, while evidence of its connections with technical schools can be seen in the strong ties that colleges still retain with industry.

This is a key feature of FE – *because* it is non-compulsory and *because* it has its roots in the Adult Education tradition, FE has come to view itself as a different offer. While FE strives to meet the needs of community and commerce, it also considers itself to be 'a second chance for people who have been failed by or who have dropped out of the system' (Foster, 2005:5). FE does not seek or try to replicate the tightly defined structures and organisation of secondary schools, acknowledging that students do not have to attend FE and even if they do attend, it is through their own free choice. FE prides itself on this difference.

The institutional culture of FE colleges today

FE has taken the opportunity to develop a different set of relationships between staff and students. FE colleges strive to uphold the principles of androgogy and mutual respect and to achieve the ideal position where contributions from the adult learner are welcomed and valued, in a 'relationship of mutual respect between teacher and learner' (Vella, 1994:182) and the tutor 'honour(s) the learner first as an adult with years of experience' (*ibid*:185). While not all tutors in all colleges achieve this ideal, it remains a cherished humanistic principle of the FE ethos.

A further significant difference between schools and FE is created by the nature of student recruitment. Schools generally have a consistent conscript population which produces little variation in student numbers. FE colleges, however, operate a system of open enrolment which can produce considerable annual fluctuations in student numbers and it is common for courses to close if insufficient numbers of students have been recruited. FE staff therefore rely on students in a way that schools do not and the relationship between student attendance and staff employment is more immediate. FE staff and students thus co-exist in a symbiotic relationship, each deriving benefit from the other: students gain an educational benefit and staff secure sustained employment. Most staff remain sharply aware of this relationship and tutor dependence on student attendance to retain their jobs.

Like all educational establishments from nursery schools to universities, FE colleges have written rules. Black students' experience of FE was colleges lacked the formal rules present in compulsory secondary schooling. Whereas schools seemed keen to enforce rules for dogmatic rather than valid educational reasons, FE colleges gave the impression of having an overt absence of rules. It is this interpretation and application of policies and procedures that have helped to produce the contemporary institutional culture of FE colleges. The contrast between schools and colleges appeared dramatic. As Michael, who was studying A-levels at one of the colleges, put it:

> Michael: I suppose the rules are cool, 'cause like the rules here are basically just like standard life rules. I don't feel like I'm restricted.

Even after studying at the college for several years students still professed little or no knowledge of the college rules despite having received a full college induction in which the rules would have been clearly explained. Other students studying on foundation level sports courses and intermediate business courses also noted this difference and made the following observations:

> Dwaine: Rules? That's the best thing. You can't exactly go on about the rules can you?
>
> Patrick: Yeah true.
>
> Clive: I don't even know the rules.
>
> Anthony: The rules?
>
> Taylor: What are the rules?
>
> SP: Well you've both been to school and you know the rules there. Does this place have lots of rules or what?

Taylor: No it's a bit laid-back innit? Not that bad really.

Tony, studying a level 1 sports course, summed up the position in the following way:

Tony: There aren't many rules.

These comments do not indicate that FE colleges have no rules. What they show is that policies and procedures were applied with care and a light hand and without the dogma students had experienced at secondary school. Students appeared to enjoy this more relaxed, adult approach which seemed to suit their needs as young and developing adults far better. This was succinctly captured by Issac, a level 2 business student:

Issac: A school leaver would fit into college a lot more, 'cause they'll understand more. It's not like they're being held down and pressured.

There was a perception among those who took part in my inquiry that school had been a stressful and controlling environment which they suffered and struggled through because they had no choice. It was not an environment they had enjoyed or which supported their development. Some Black boys had experienced school as 'a kind of warfare' (Fordham, 1996:283) where they found themselves embattled or permanently under siege, constantly needing to defend themselves against attack from staff and students.

The perceived absence of excessive or unreasonable rules in colleges produced an entirely different institutional culture: a culture that relied on students managing and taking control of their own behaviour rather than having to follow orders; a culture that was prepared to risk giving students responsibility for their own actions; a culture that was willing, at least initially, to trust students. For some Black boys and men, the school staff who were fulfilling their controlling function became oppressors or virtual gaolers instead of tutors. In this sense schools became transformed into a 'prison' (Sewell, 1997:42) from which they wanted to escape; a place where they were detained against their will; a place where co-operation was obtained through compulsion rather than choice. This was summarised by level 2 business students Taylor and Anthony and Curtis, a level 2 arts student:

Taylor: School was more strict than this.

Anthony: Most of the teachers never shout here.

Taylor: Basically you can leave college when you want. It's definitely not strict. You can drop out and stuff. You couldn't do that at school could you?

Curtis: The atmosphere. It's well cool.

Despite the apparently casual approach to rules and discipline, Black students appreciated the need for and existence of college rules, which on occasions would need to be enforced. However, they believed the way college tutors enforced rules was very different from schools. They viewed college tutors as impartial arbitrators who avoided unnecessary interrogation and sought both sides of a story before reaching conclusions or taking action. This view was cogently expressed by Gregory, Clark, Joseph and Lawrence who were studying a level 1 sports course, and Abraham who was studying A levels:

> Gregory: Listen to my side?
>
> Clark: Most of the time.
>
> Joseph: Yeah. Just say me and you had an argument. They aint going to listen to me and not listen to you. They'd get both sides.
>
> Lawrence: Of course.
>
> Abraham: We really don't get them people grilling you in college.

Black students found further evidence of the informal and relaxed approach of colleges in the way college tutors allowed students to address staff, and the way college tutors chose in turn to speak to students. Isaac, a level 2 business student explained it like this:

> Issac: That's what makes it better than school as well. You can talk to teachers without saying 'Sir', or having to talk to them like they're all high. 'Cause the teachers here are on the same level if you know what I mean.

This egalitarian approach was significant for Black students. Other research (Sewell, 1997; Gillborn, 2008; Byfield, 2008) has shown that Black students in secondary school regularly reported being on the receiving end of unfair treatment, to the point where they felt that their teachers simply 'did not care about them' (Blair and Bourne, 1998:85). Secondary schools had become an unrelenting litany of antagonism and hostility between staff and students. Being allowed to call tutors by their first names signalled a cultural shift between schools and colleges and helped to reinforce the ideology that colleges were places where students were valued as equal partners (Jarvis, 2005), in contrast to the strict hierarchical organisation of schools where students were, as a matter of course, viewed as less significant and less important than teachers and other staff.

The way that college tutors worked with students during taught sessions was also different. When studying in college, Black students found most taught classes to be characterised by a relaxed and friendly atmosphere where staff and students could share a joke with each other in a reciprocally respectful environment. And their college tutors were comfortable in using 'appropriate and timely humour' (Kher, Molstad and Donahue, 1999:400) to help support teaching. This use of humour was noted by the students including Isaac:

> Issac: I'd say that I've had a laugh in lessons. I still do. I have a laugh with the teachers and what not.

Three level 2 art students also commented on their appreciation of the tutors' light touch:

> Stephen: You can have a joke in class, a joke or whatever, and in that way you're enjoying the work more. And you're more awake instead of just being dry and quiet and dull where you're falling asleep.
>
> Curtis: Most of the time we get jokes. It's a good laugh
>
> Stephen: We've had quite a bit of joke since we've been here
>
> Angus: College is a great laugh

Using humour and sharing jokes was seen as a significant factor in producing the institutional culture of colleges. The stress-free approach helped to reinforce the more liberal working practices of colleges where having a laugh and a joke together was seen as an acceptable working practice which supported the achievement of positive learning outcomes. As these level 1 sports students said:

> Paul: You can have a laugh in that lesson.
>
> Kevin: It's exciting, funny. We liven it up.

Ofsted have endorsed this approach to learning, noting that staff/student conversations that were 'lightened by humour' (2002:10) were needed to achieve a thriving learning climate. Other research has shown how laughter can be used to 'forge better relationships and to create an atmosphere judged to be conducive to the achievement of the aims of the school' (Woods, 1976: 178). When used productively, humour was capable of cultivating 'freer interaction, idea generation and group cohesiveness, while reducing anxiety, conformity and dogmatism' (Korobkin, 1988:155). However, many Black students had not enjoyed such humour while at school and any laughter was 'a reaction against authority and routine' (*ibid*). Moreover, when Black students experienced teachers having a joke at school it was more often perceived as being aggressive and disrespectful towards them and their culture or, as one student explained in other research:

Keith: Those so-called jokes, were no joke, you were being cheeky. I went home and told my mum and she said that if you say it again she would come and sort you out. As for that girl, if it was my father, he wouldn't just take you to the CRE, he would also give you a good thump. My father says that a teacher should set a good example for the children by respecting each one, whether Black or White. (Eggleston *et al*, 1986:131)

Significantly these comments also appear to reveal an undercurrent of racist humour in schools, the sort of humour which 'creates a hostile learning environment that quickly stifles communication' (Kher, Molstad and Donahue 1999:402). Black students confirmed that this kind of aggressive humour was absent in colleges and that jokes were mutually enjoyed by staff and students and were not an instrument of control or humiliation.

The collective impact of the perceived absence of dogma and imposed hierarchies, along with an informal atmosphere supported by humour, produced a relaxed and safe ethos for Black students, leading them to observe that, in contrast to their generally negative school experience, colleges were places where:

Peter: There's always stuff poppin'. (Level 1 sports student)

Within a contemporary context, in which Black men and boys are regularly negatively portrayed as adopting 'a ritualised form of masculinity which openly seeks confrontation' (Majors and Billson, 1992:4), a positive youth culture which actively seeks 'poppin' events counters popularised imagery which portray Black men as 'gangsters [and] drug smugglers' and 'panders to existing racial stereotypes' (Maylor *et al*, 2006:64). In contrast students believed colleges provided a friendly environment for staff and learners alike:

Joseph: I've never come to college and felt unsafe or that there's someone out to get me, or no-one's going to talk to me, or teachers stressing my case.

(Level 1 sports student)

Stephen: You don't see no beef around.

Curtis: You know nuff people innit. You always see someone. You can always talk to someone. It's not like you walk the corridors and there's no-one to talk to.

(Level 2 art students)

Bhattacharyya *et al*, too, found that the majority of colleges were successful in providing opportunities for young Black men 'to develop positive relationships with tutors who (were) perceived to care about the progress and well-being of young people' (2003:24). These findings combine to suggest that college staff had successfully identified ways to promote positive relationships with Black men and boys which were founded on mutual trust and respect. This was in stark contrast to the findings of the London Development Agency who found that in schools ...

> the degree of care experienced by African-Caribbean pupils from their teachers, the quality of communication with their teachers, and levels of conflict with teachers, was all less positive for African-Caribbean boys than for boys from most other groups. (2004:8)

The BBC similarly reported that Black pupils in schools were 'held back by a lack of support and a negative stereotype of Black schoolchildren held by some teachers' (BBC news online, May 2003). In their research Blair and Bourne noted some White teachers 'had problems relating to Black students, a problem which existed whether or not Black students reacted to teachers' (1998:85). While these negative examples of staff/student relationships are not presented as the definitive experience for every Black pupil in all secondary schools, they are indicative of the significant differences that exist between the two sectors. Collectively they present a persuasive argument that the learning environment of FE is more suitable for and receptive to the learning needs of Black men and boys than that of schools.

The overall friendliness of colleges was so significant that students believed college was like a home to them, to the extent that it eliminated the need to participate in a 'relentless performance for the mainstream audience' (Maylor *et al*, 2006:64). This again, was in stark contrast to their secondary school experience as noted by two level 1 sports students:

> Joseph: To me, the college is like a home. It's like a second home to me. So I recommend my course and college to a lot of people.

> John: College is like a home. College is like a second home to me, or I should say first home 'cause I spend more time in college than what I do at home. It's like a home really.

In addition to their liberal approach to classroom and student management, some college tutors went further to create a different atmosphere, playing background music during teaching. Women tutors did not become agitated or aggrieved at being called 'love' or 'darling'. School teachers rarely play music during any lesson, with the possible exceptions of art or drama, and background music would not routinely be considered compatible with academic theory sessions. Nor would it usually be R Kelly, Tupac or Chicane, which students could relate to and identify with. Here is another clear division between colleges and schools, another way in which learning is promoted and supported by college staff.

That college students were comfortable about to call a tutor 'love' or 'darling' is also significant. The women tutors gave the impression they would rather concentrate on student learning or, if necessary, more significant behavioural issues. This approach minimised the significance of the comments and avoided confrontation. Thus staff attention was not directed towards relatively minor misdemeanours associated with hierarchical structures and staff could concentrate on supporting students in completing their work or managing more serious transgressions.

Another possible interpretation of the students' language connects with their feeling 'at home' within the college environment and an almost familial attachment to their tutors, so they began to use terms of address that would ordinarily be reserved for family members or female friends.

The secure atmosphere of colleges was also significant to this group of students and prompted one level 2 business student to say:

> Moses: People aren't here to fight. The atmosphere, you can just tell. People are just here to do whatever they're doing. Like make friends or whatever. Everyone's laid back man.

For Black students, college provided more than courses that would help them gain employment or the opportunity to progress to higher level study, they also served a wider social function where learners made new friends, as described here:

> Clement: Even if you didn't know them before college, at least you've made friends.
>
> (A level student)
>
> Joseph: Basically my life now is college. I've got a few friends outside college but I don't really see them much or get involved with them any more. So basically college is my life really.
>
> (Level 1 sports student)

However, of all the factors which produced the institutional culture of colleges, it was being treated as an adult that the Black students responded to most positively and valued most highly. This was possibly because it contrasted sharply with their school experiences and signified a complete change in organisational culture. These comments from students are telling:

Angus: You're treated differently from schools. More like adults.

Curtis: Yeah, you get a bit more respect. That's it really.

SP: Is that a good thing, getting a bit more respect?

Angus: When you're in school, like basically, you just get treated like kids. College is different.

(Level 2 art students)

Joseph: All the teachers here are safe.

Clark: Yeah.

SP: Why? What's the difference?

Joseph: They treat you more mature. They treat you like adults. That's what I think anyway.

SP: Did they treat you like adults at school?

Joseph: No. I don't think so.

(Level 1 sports students)

Clement: Yeah, I do feel respected. I don't get treated like a child. I get treated on the same level as teachers, and I value certain teachers as friends as well.

(A level student)

Ofsted noted this positive relationship in their 2005 survey of FE colleges, which records students' comments about the 'friendly and supportive teachers, the safe and secure environment, the way they were treated with respect as individuals, and the support and opportunities they were provided' (2005:4).

During teaching sessions college tutors reinforced the more relaxed adult nature of colleges by commonly adopting the following classroom procedures:

- Customary formal structures were not imposed – registers were not called out, students were allowed into classes without first lining up outside the room and there was no requirement to call the tutor Sir, Mr, Miss or Mrs.
- Students were routinely allowed to sit where they chose unless there was a specific learning need to formulate groups in a specific way. There were no seating plans.
- Students were allowed to take cold drinks into lessons.

- Tutors were tolerant of calling out in class and did not insist that students raise their hands to make contributions.
- Tutors were flexible about time keeping and no sanctions were applied if students were less than ten minutes late for a session.
- Most colleges do not have a blanket uniform policy, as they recognised the diversity and adult status of their students.

Although each of these measures may appear insignificant in isolation, their combined effect created an entirely different institutional atmosphere to school and declared in FE, things *are* different. The style changed from control by direction and coercion to control by negotiation and consent. This was *the* difference that made FE a new educational experience and gave students a new and alternative way to learn.

The Black students who took part in my research consequently felt a strong sense of affinity towards FE. This was not simply a result of the amount of time they had been at college, and although many students had attended their schools for a comparable time they had no similar feelings of connection. The Black students felt college deserved their loyalty because of the opportunities and chances it had given to them – opportunities that some of them believed they had been denied at school.

However, although most of the students had a positive experience of learning at college, valued being treated like an adult and enjoyed their new found respect some of them struggled with having to study alongside older students and found adjusting to a different and 'more 'mature' atmosphere' (FEU, 1987:7) challenging. A Level 1 sports student summarised this ambivalence:

> Patrick: There's more older people in class. So you'll get people who are like 19, 20 in your class, you get socialised with adults. At school it's more like your own age.

> SP: So is it a bad thing having older people in the class?

> Patrick: It's not a bad thing, but you feel more comfortable around your own age.

An A level student recognised, however, that the presence of older learners probably produced a hidden bonus in that tutors would feel obliged to accord the same level of respect to younger learners when they were being taught alongside older students.

> Abraham: They've got to treat everybody equally. Treating everybody equally here means you've gotta treat us the same as the older students. Like you've

got people who are 60 and 70 as well as 16 year olds. So you have to give certain respect and make them feel more like adults. I like the way I'm treated at college. It's one of the main reasons I came to college, to be treated like an adult.

It is unlikely that colleges which have their roots in the Mechanics' Institutes of the nineteenth century and the Adult Learning Sector of the twentieth century are ever likely to discourage older learners from attending their programmes so the challenge for some younger Black students of having to learn alongside older learners in the same class is likely to remain.

Conclusion

This chapter has described the many positive aspects of college culture. In many ways FE, like the Mechanics' Institutes before them has retained a schizophrenic personality, split between different agendas, responding to different pressures and trying to balance them all in an uneasy and sometimes difficult alliance. To this day colleges are still, as Foster observes 'striking in their heterogeneity. They deliver in a wide variety of settings and the range of learning opportunities they present is extraordinary' (2005:8).

It was this choice and variety that Black men and boys found to be one of the most attractive features of FE. In addition, they particularly appreciated the absence of formality, strict rules and rigid hierarchal structures that characterise schools. The relaxed and informal atmosphere was more suited to their learning needs, although some students expressed unease about having to learn alongside older people. However, everyone who participated in my research project was unanimous that the atmosphere and culture of FE colleges was not only different from schools, it was far better.

In summary, although FE colleges show similarities with secondary schools in terms of size and of curriculum delivery that is organised by subject, they counter the potentially harmful effects of their organisation through their positive and productive staff/student relationships. This key difference has produced the distinct institutional culture of FE, an institutional culture which is far more suited to the needs of Black men and boys (Bhattacharyya *et al*, 2003; BBC, 2003; Ofsted, 2005; London Development Agency, 2004).

4

The academic organisation of FE

Introduction

Whereas schools have a statutory National Curriculum, 'there is no single curriculum specification for further education' (Cantor, Roberts and Pratley, 1995:48). 'The wide-ranging needs of students, employers and other users and the diversity of the sector's response to them makes it difficult to talk of a single further education curriculum' (Frankel and Reeves, 1996:11). These authors describe the FE curriculum as the 'untidy residue of the curricula of other institutions' (*ibid*), a curriculum that is not readily or easily classified. And while provision in FE is now more tightly controlled since the 1992 Act, the curriculum of FE can still be seen as elective in that if a subject exists at all it exists because there is a direct demand from consumers.

The National Curriculum for schools has produced a prescribed set of curriculum choices (QCA, 2007) for most pupils. Even in years 10 and 11 when they are mostly studying their option choices at GCSE or other levels, they are generally obliged to follow a compulsory core of mathematics, English and science. Some have their choices further reduced by being directed to study certain options. Other researchers have identified the curriculum as a major contributing factor to Black student underachievement because it fails to recognise cultural diversity and has promoted a Eurocentric view of the world (Cassidy, 2005; Hall, 2005). This has prevented Black students from developing 'knowledge about their cultural heritage' (Bagley and Coard, 1975:322) and schools have therefore been encouraged to re-examine their curriculum and to incorporate multicultural and antiracist perspectives.

The taught curriculum within the FE sector is identical to that within the statutory sector and students study for and sit the same examinations and assessments. This curriculum must therefore be the same curriculum as criticised by Hall and Cassidy which has denied Black students an opportunity to develop an understanding of their cultural heritage and has been identified as one cause of their low academic achievement. Yet in FE 'particular underachieving groups were showing positive results' (Ofsted, 2005:17). Ofsted also noted that 'in effective colleges with low proportions of ethnic minority learners, close attention to the needs of individual learners achieved good results' (*ibid*). This shows a reversal of the trend evident in many secondary schools and so questions whether the curriculum itself has a negative impact on Black students.

The FE curriculum

A key difference between school and college was in the students' perception of choice. School students felt they had too little choice regarding subjects they had to study but did not link this limitation to the statutory requirements of the national curriculum and key stage four, viewing it instead as a repressive measure. Colleges have an in-built advantage over schools, as they can allow the students a greater degree of choice in their studies. As these A level students at college saw it:

> Abraham: You didn't get a choice whether you could do technology or not. I hated being in school for them reasons.
>
> Int: So the choice was too restricted?
>
> Abraham: It was definitely too restricted.
>
> Gary: Definitely.
>
> Abraham: Now you come to college and you want to do this, this, this and this and they say 'Well this is your timetable' – Done. And if you can't do certain things you've always got a big, vast selection you can choose from after that anyway, so if you can't do this, you can do this.

The greater freedom of choice that colleges were able to offer meant the students felt more in control of their learning. From the start they were far more motivated than they were while at school. The Black men and boys who participated in this inquiry approached their studies far more positively as a consequence:

> SP: How do you find the curriculum here at college?

John: It's not perfect. No it's perfect but it's not 100 per cent spot on. With college you more or less get your choice of what you want to learn because you look through the manual, and you read about your course. When I read about this first diploma course I seen everything that it involved so I picked it. That's just the same with everybody

Clive: 'Cause I've chosen things myself it's more varied 'cause I've chosen things I'm interested in. It comes down to the choices I've made

Clark: In college you make your own decisions

(Level 1 sports students)

Such positive motivation was typical of the students who took part in this study and overall they enjoyed being liberated from what they perceived as the rigid constraints of their school timetables. They also thought the college had a more appealing and relevant choice of subject opportunities. This positive attitude spilled over into other curriculum areas, so even if the course design obliged them to take less favoured subjects they still engaged in a positive fashion, stating that:

Taylor: Even if it's boring it's still meaningful

Anthony: I wouldn't be here if it was a waste of time. I'd have left the first day if I felt that way.

(Level 2 business students)

These comments seemed to illustrate the students' developing maturity in enabling them to accept even 'boring' subjects as being academically useful. Additionally the students appreciated the efforts made by staff to heighten the relevance of other subjects by making links to their chosen vocational areas of study. Two level 1 sports students told me:

Joseph: But it's not boring because they involve it. It's like I'm doing sports BTEC, and all the maths and English all involve something to do with sports. Like in English if I'm doing any writing up it will be a session plan. It's all to do with what we're doing in college – all the numeracy and communications and stuff. I think it's good because it involves what we're doing

Clark: Even maths is relevant 'cause it's all about sports

The initial opportunity to exercise choice and to shape their own programme encouraged the students to grapple with some of the more challenging areas of the curriculum, which they now viewed as areas for development rather than as an unwelcome and unwarranted academic imposition. One A level student said:

Abraham: You're like engaged with the topic. Even though some of it's hard to get your head round, it's quite interesting.

However, while Black men and boys agreed the college curriculum was more relevant and interesting than their school curriculum, they were not entirely satisfied. They thought there was room for further improvement, especially when they believed some aspects of the school curriculum were replicated in the college. This was particularly true of the requirement by the college that students continue to study literacy and numeracy if they had not already attained a pass at GCSE of C or above. This made them feel the work was being repeated and they found it boring:

Clive: It seems we're covering the same stuff from school, but in more detail

(Level 1 sports student)

Stephen: The thing is we've been learning the same thing like years. It's just too long.

(Level 2 art student)

Further difficulties were created when one college tutor lacked the appropriate communication skills to convey subject information in an engaging manner, as these level 2 business students told me:

Moses: Sometimes the way the teacher explains something. It's just boring innit?

Barry: Basically, right, there could be better ways to put certain points across that are being taught that would make it more exciting. Something that we can relate to.

Moses: But he will relate it to something he knows about, and that's it.

These students' comments indicated the tutor's restricted communication skills and also his inability to select examples that related to students' needs. Even though Moses had assessed this particular tutor as 'boring', he later stated:

Moses: Yeah, he is a good teacher. I'm not going to fault him, 'cause I did get a merit. Yeah I got a merit, but I didn't understand what I was talking about.

This final comment indicated that despite communication difficulties, the tutor had successfully established a productive student rapport with the student and this was valued. But this tutor still found it difficult to enable the student to fully understand the work and to open up the curriculum in a meaningful fashion. However, it was also possible this student did not want to appear to be a high achiever in front of his peer group, and had purposely presented himself as failing to understand.

Black students repeatedly criticised the college curriculum because sessions were so long. Most of them believed the standard two-hour session was excessive. Black students had sufficient self awareness to recognise that they could not stay engaged for this length of time and that their attention wandered. They talked about their long teaching sessions in the following way:

John: The day just drags.

Andrew: You get two 2-hour lessons.

John: And the day just drags forever, forever.

(Level 1 sports students)

Anthony: It's only boring when they're like two hours long.

(Level 2 business student)

As Teachernet observes, 'adults find it quite difficult to concentrate with unbroken attention for much more than about 20 minutes, for younger learners the concentration span is much less' and 'there is clear evidence that learners concentrate and learn more from short, focused activities' (Teachernet, online). So it is not surprising that many of the Black students reported that they found the two hour sessions irksome and tiresome.

One college tutor dealt with the specific issue of overlong sessions by focusing on task achievement and allowed the students to engage in other activities as long as they had completed the work they had been given. She adopted a potentially controversial classroom management strategy, being prepared for students in her class to work in time-limited blocks, so that no learning activity lasted longer than 20 minutes and learning breaks were a scheduled part of the lesson. Further, she did not insist that students behaved as though they were productively engaged with tasks if they were not. Instead, her focus was on the outcome at the end of the session. She believed that many students, Black and White, struggled to stay engaged for long sessions because of their concentration spans and recognised that the expectations of their endurance were unrealistic.

Many of the Black students became even more dissatisfied when the long sessions involved writing because they did not appreciate the connection of written work with satisfactory completion of the programme. This negative orientation towards writing is consistent with differences 'between boys and girls in language and literacy skills' (DfES, 2007:5), where girls consistently outperform their male counterparts in written tasks. This is not a new phenomenon, and has been evidenced 'from historical data from English exam records going back 60 years' (*ibid*). So it was not surprising that some of them openly admitted how they had struggled with writing and found it dull:

> Joseph: 'Cause writing can get boring. The work itself is good.
>
> Clark: It's the fact of doing the writing. That's boring innit.
>
> SP: Anything in particular that's boring?
>
> Gregory: The writing.
>
> (Level 1 sports students)

If colleges have a goal of enhancing curriculum relevance and increasing student engagement, statements like these present a serious challenge to traditional teaching methods. If they wish to increase engagement, colleges and awarding bodies need to actively consider different methods for students to record their work and employ alternative assessment techniques. Only in this way can students be released from the burden of excessive writing and this would be beneficial for all students, Black and White alike, and may help to keep male students engaged with their work.

In a final challenge to the college curriculum, some students said they believed colleges failed to deliver adequate stimulation and variety for the duration of some programmes. This led these level 1 sports students to comment:

> Andrew: Like at the beginning of college I reckon it was good because you're getting to know new people, but now it's coming to the middle, it's like the same thing.
>
> John: It's like the same old on a different day.

While the participants reported that they experienced decreasing levels of stimulation as the programme progressed, this could also be indicative of their own unrealistic expectations. However, even though some students had difficulty in maintaining interest for the duration of a college programme, all made it clear that they enjoyed the informal atmosphere and the way the college tutors worked with them, to the point that in many sessions their college tutors were integrated within the teaching group and were sometimes indistinguishable from the student population. Many college tutors appeared to have consciously decided to do all they could to remove or minimise barriers between them and all the learners so they could work more closely with them.

Although the participants agreed that there were many positive features in the college curriculum, the initial statement of one student that the curriculum was 'perfect, but not 100 per cent spot on' was not echoed by every Black student and was probably overly optimistic. Many students suggested possible improvements to the college curriculum regarding, for instance, the length of sessions and the traditional method of recording and assessing work. However, the initial positive endorsement of the college curriculum remains important, for it shows the immense difference in the students' perception of the school and college curricula. This difference in perception cannot be on account of content or the mode of delivery, as these are much the same as in schools. They relate to the college ethos and the opportunity to influence the subjects studied. It was the informal, adult and mutually respectful environment of college and student choice which helped to make the curriculum more palatable for the students.

Black boys' achievements on their programmes

A significant feature of any students' academic experience while studying is whether or not they pass the course they have enrolled on. Although the DES publishes national league tables indicating the academic achievement of students of all ethnicities in secondary schools, data indicating the academic success of Black students in FE has not and still is not released to the general public in the same way. However, individual colleges can access data on student success rates from the Skills Funding Agency (SFA) which provides details of student achievement organised by ethnicity, age, gender and any declared disability, similar to the statistics provided by the DES. Student success rates are calculated by multiplying the percentage of students completing the course by the percentage of students who gained the principal qualification they had enrolled for. Prior to 2008 this service was carried out by the Learning and Skills Council (LSC).

We now look at information supplied by the LSC on the academic achievement of the students who attended the urban college in comparison to overall student achievement. The data from the college shows student success rates for three successive years, 2003-04, 2004-05 and 2005-06. The students who took part in this study are located in the Black African, Black Caribbean and Black Other categories for 2005-06. Twenty-three of the research participants were aged 16-18 and the remaining three were 19 or over. This information indicated how well Black students were performing in relation to other ethnic groups studying on similar programmes. Because of the sensitive nature of this data and micro political agendas, the suburban college chose not to make similar data available.

Student success rates from 2003 to 2006

The following tables show the student success rate by age and ethnicity at the urban college. The first table presents data for 16-18 year olds; the second for students aged 19 and over; and the third table shows aggregated data of all Black students compared to White.

Ethnicity	Academic Year					
	2003-04		2004-05		2005-06	
	No	Success Rate %	No	Success Rate %	No	Success Rate %
Any Other	39	64	41	63	38	89
Bangladeshi	2	0	12	75	12	67
Black African	31	45	33	67	51	75
Black Caribbean	177	46	171	64	176	57
Black Other	20	55	24	33	34	68
Chinese	12	67	7	86	3	33
Indian	86	42	76	51	84	63
Mixed	127	9	197	53	251	70
Other Asian	9	67	5	80	11	82
Pakistani	120	53	114	50	83	47
Unknown	178	65	101	73	28	64
White	2578	61	2425	69	2285	74
Total	3379		3206		3057	

Table 3: Success Rates of 16-18 Year Old Students by Ethnicity from 2003 to 2006 for the Urban College

In the 16-18 age group the only Black group which consistently improved over the three year period were Black African students whose success rates increased from 45 per cent to 67 per cent to 75 per cent as shown in Table 3. The achievement of two other groups, Black Caribbean and Black Other, followed no identifiable pattern. For the 19 plus age group both Black Caribbean and other Black students showed consistent improvement, while the achievement of Black African students slightly declined over the three years. The students who participated in my research project all achieved on the programmes for which they were enrolled. This admittedly small group achieved a 100 per cent success rate. The achievement of these students is shown in the overall success rate figure for 2005-06.

Ethnicity	Academic Year					
	2003-04		2004-05		2005-06	
	No	Success Rate %	No	Success Rate %	No	Success Rate %
Any Other	227	48	256	58	198	75
Bangladeshi	9	56	21	76	15	47
Black African	122	69	103	66	116	66
Black Caribbean	272	60	250	65	252	67
Black Other	44	64	39	72	57	74
Chinese	80	44	51	63	65	69
Indian	272	58	199	63	172	78
Mixed	180	64	163	67	202	71
Other Asian	76	59	79	75	66	86
Pakistani	282	53	249	70	197	59
Unknown	2981	81	1544	81	774	82
White	15193	74	12367	79	9321	82
Total	19738		15321		11435	

Table 4: Success Rates of 19+ Year Old Students by Ethnicity from 2003 to 2006 for the Urban College

Group	Academic Year					
	2003-04		2004-05		2005-06	
	Success Rate %	% Gap in Success Rates relative to White Peers	Success Rate %	% Gap in Success Rates relative to White Peers	Success Rate %	% Gap in Success Rates relative White Peers
All 16-18 Black Groups	49	12	55	14	67	7
All 19+ Black Groups	64	10	68	11	69	13
All 16-18 White Groups	61	-	69	-	74	-
All 19+ White Groups	74	-	79	-	82	-

Table 5: Aggregated Achievement of All Black Students Compared to White Students from 2003 to 2006 for the Urban College

Source: LSC Student Success Rates Report 2006

Only in one year did any Black 16-18 year old group outperform their White counterparts. In 2005-06, Black African students achieved a success rate of 75 per cent compared to 74 per cent for White students. For all other years, all other Black groups across the age range persistently performed worse than their White counterparts. However, if achievement scores of all three Black groups are aggregated, both 16-18 year olds and 19+ students show a modest improvement in success rates over the period, as shown in Table 5. But it must be remembered these figures have been enhanced by the consistently high success rates of Black African students and that they also included data for Black females, who consistently show higher achievement rates than their male peers. While this data appears to suggest an overall improvement with time, the finding needs to be treated with some caution, because if the achievement gap relative to White peers is examined, it is evident that there has not been a consistent year-on-year reduction in the gap between them. Moreover, the picture regarding Black student achievement relative to their White counterparts becomes even less clear, as it is evident that White students have also improved their success rates during this time.

It is important to remember that all the Black students who participated in this research project passed the course they had enrolled on. The impact of such success needs to be taken into account: being successful, this group may have perceived and reported their experience of FE differently from the way less successful Black peers might have done. It is also possible that their academic success was not wholly attributable to the FE experience. They might have arrived at college with positive attitudes to study which continued while they were at college and contributed to their overall positive experience of FE. We cannot, therefore, know whether their perceptions would have been the same if they had been less successful in their studies.

Conclusion

The data provided in this chapter has described the views of Black men and boys towards the curriculum they encountered in colleges and their levels of academic attainment relative to their White peers. In the schools sector, national data has shown that the achievement levels for Black students have improved over time and they are obtaining greater numbers of qualifications at higher grades. Significantly, however, Black students' levels of academic attainment have consistently been lower than those of their White peers and they remain one of the lowest achieving groups of all ethnicities in the schools sector.

National data for student achievement in FE is limited and data has not been collected and reported in the same way as for schools. National research completed by Ofsted from 2002-2004 (see Chapter 2) has shown that on transferring to FE, Black students experienced greater success in obtaining sought after academic qualifications. However, despite these improvements, the same data also indicated a lower level of academic achievement by Black groups relative to other ethnic groups.

Data collected for this research project indicated that perceptually Black men and boys had a more positive and enjoyable experience of the curriculum offered in college than they had done at school. For the students who participated in my research this translated into academic achievement and successful course completion. However, as the data only covered a three year period and looked at a relatively small group, it was insufficient to determine conclusively whether all Black males studying in FE achieved better academic results than those studying at schools.

PART THREE
ROUTES TO SUCCESS

5

The influence of race on learning

Introduction

Within the context of poor academic achievement and being identified as at best an outsider and at worst as an aggressive assailant, Black males face a choice – will they conform to imposed racialised stereotypes or will they present an alternative construction of themselves? Personal presentation for all Black students at all levels in education remains an ongoing issue. Black men and boys can consciously and deliberately choose to influence how they are perceived by others or leave their public presentation to chance. Whether the choice is controlled and orchestrated or not, Black men and boys are judged by the wider community on their actions and these will either confirm existing unforgiving stereotypes or challenge prevailing imagery and perceptions of Black masculinity.

Much of the media portrays Black men and boys as either 'super athlete, criminal, gangster or hypersexual male' (Swanson, Cunningham and Spencer, 2003:609). It is against this background that Black men and boys find themselves measured not on their academic abilities but on preconceived stereotypes which are governed by their racial identity. Guilt is conferred by the media suggestion that Black males as a group can only be successful in a physical sense or are bad, and that all Black men and boys without exception fit into this category. It is not the person who is seen but an image of Black masculinity. By default, all Black men and boys are assumed to behave and act in a fashion predetermined by this stereotype. There is no recognition of individuality or difference and Black males are viewed as a homogenous indistinguishable mass where the 'diversity and heterogeneity that has marked British culture throughout' (Westwood, 1989:1) is ignored.

Presentations of Black masculinity within education

Although Black boys have been demonised as they grow into men, this negative image does not exist when they begin their primary school education. In his research Grant showed that 'upon entering school in primary grades, Black children possess enthusiasm and eager interest' (1992:17). Yet this positive representation does not continue and at some indeterminate time before they transfer to secondary school, the perception of Black boys is replaced by the damaging stereotypes already described and teachers become 'content to live with general 'impressions' or 'hunches'' about Black boys (Ofsted, 1999: 7). The teachers' acceptance of these stereotypes results in their expecting underperformance or resistance from Black boys. Consequently, by the time they enter secondary schools, Black boys are compelled to make a conscious or unconscious decision regarding the image they will present and behaviour they will adopt – choosing either to conform to imposed negative and destructive stereotypes or to resist such images and pursue scholarly activities.

To survive in a fundamentally antagonistic environment, Black students have had to develop certain strategies to support their survival. While some choose to reject mainstream education, not all do so. Consequently 'even if few in number, there are students who manage to maintain their identities and achieve academically' (Noguera, 2003:446). However, as he points out:

> we know much less about resilience and perseverance and the coping strategies employed by individuals whose lives are surrounded by hardships than we do about those who succumb and become victims of their environment. (*ibid*:438)

While in education, Black students present in ways that can be divided into three distinct categories. They are either challengers, chameleons or resistors.

Each of these strategies presents Black learners with a number of potential hazards from both the education system and from their peers, both Black and White.

	Category		
	Challengers	Chameleons	Resistors
Strategy	Rude-boy	Overt accommodators	Academic agitators
	Cool-Pose	Covert accommodators	Guerrillas

Table 6: Survival strategies in education

Challengers

Rude-boy

Some Black students have chosen to conform to the rude-boy stereotype so 'are more likely to act out in the classroom' (Noguera, 2003:437) and present challenging or openly aggressive behaviour in school or college. In his work in UK secondary schools, Sewell (1997) found teachers believed many Black boys willingly donned the mantle of the stereotypical belligerent, under-achieving Black male.

Adopting a rude-boy style was and still is the approach most likely to create difficulties between teachers and students. Sewell (1997) found approximately 90 per cent of the teaching staff in one school were either openly antagonistic towards or irritated by the perceived macho-posturing of Black boys. Teachers could not cope with their behaviour and believed they acted in this way to maintain their street credibility or enhance their image amongst other Black students. Teachers believed that Black boys were more interested in being 'anointed 'cool' ' (Connor, 2003:31) or gaining positive 'social regard' (Wickline, 2003:9) from their Black peers rather than in pursuing 'White-sanctioned values such as academic achievement' (Wickline, 2003:9). Being a rude-boy secured membership of a recognised Black cultural group and ensured close contact with others who belonged to it. This presentation has been closely associated with antisocial behaviour. As one A level student in my research observed:

> Michael: The image is sometimes to stereotype people with the hoods and with the hats. People who commit crimes and stuff like wear that sort of clothes. If you wear that style of clothes you're gonna be stereotyped.

Michael recognised that dressing in a certain style and being Black con-firmed, for some teachers, an assumed criminality.

'Cool pose'

'Cool pose' (Majors *et al*, 1992:1) has become 'the norm for most young Black males between the ages of ten and twenty' (hooks, 2001:42). Black boys 'assume facades of high self-esteem, aloofness and calmness' (Wickline, 2003: 9). This presentation has enabled Black boys to simultaneously distance them-selves from and question the value of mainstream education. When failure is a predicted outcome, 'Cool pose' has given Black youth protection, for there can be no shame in failing in a devalued and irrelevant education system.

'Cool pose' can also be interpreted as defiance. Although it lacks the overt aggression of the rude-boy presentation, it is dismissive of authority and authority figures. 'Cool pose' mannerisms caused teachers intangible irritation. Ms Williams in Sewell's study said:

> The Black pupils act in a particular way. The way they challenge authority is very different to the way the White pupils challenge authority. They do it in a particular style. It is the same way they relate to each other and this comes out of their sub-culture. (1997:36)

Even though there was no obvious aggression, the 'particular way' Black boys chose to act in school, caused offence to their teachers because it represented a direct challenge to structural authority, and by implication to White mainstream culture and White teachers. Through their actions Black boys accentuated their ethnicity and refused to be assimilated into the dominant White hegemonic culture. This rejection and repudiation of White culture created antagonism between Black boys and teaching staff because the students were not just refusing to conform, they were signalling their denunciation of and indifference to White culture and values.

'Cool pose' can also be interpreted as a judicious response to an education system which has denied opportunities to Black people and 'circumscribed their ambitions' (Allen, 2006:13), a system in which many Black boys have become used to being singled out for unfair treatment (Eggleston *et al*, 1986; Polite, 1994; Solorzano *et al*, 2000; Blair, 2001). In this scenario, 'cool pose' represents a logical response to an unfair and oppressive regime in which Black boys can never expect to be treated or rewarded fairly no matter how hard they work. In this situation, 'cool pose' is not an emotional reaction but a rational choice based on perceived facts and knowledge.

While most formulations of 'cool pose' represent a negative reaction to traditional education, it also has a positive function, enabling Black men and boys to signal their legitimate membership of Black culture by denying White mainstream values and standards. In this regard 'cool pose' is consistent with Maslow's (1943) hierarchy of needs in which 'belongingness needs have predominance over esteem and achievement needs' (Wickline, 2003:9).

Although 'cool pose' may have social capital among other Black students, allowing them to gain or retain cultural integrity among their Black peers, it is an inherently perilous strategy. 'Cool pose', by its very nature, seeks to accentuate the differences between Black learners, mainstream education and wider society beyond. It thus formulates Black men and boys as outsiders to an education system in which they do not belong and have no place. To adopt a 'cool pose' means, by definition, choosing to disengage with certain sectors of society. And this means relying solely upon the support and reserves of the Black community. In this monoculture, populated only by other members of the Black community, 'cool pose' is no longer a reaction to conditions, it becomes a way of life. However, those who choose to operate outside the system may find it difficult to navigate a path back into the system at a later stage. Effectively, adopting a 'cool pose' puts Black boys at risk of becoming permanent outsiders to mainstream society.

Chameleons
Open accommodators

Other Black boys and men have chosen to navigate education by taking on conventional mannerisms which subscribe 'to accepted school norms' (Rhamie and Hallam, 2002:159) and adopt the 'means and goals' of schools (Sewell, 2004:104). This could involve any number of changes to behaviour, including modifying their dress, speech and demeanour. Figueroa and Nehaul describe a student who 'learned to speak like the English in college' (1999:14), as a way of surviving and accessing education. Similarly, hooks, reflecting on her education observed how 'if one was not from a privileged class group, adopting a demeanour similar to that of the group could help one to advance' (1994:178).

I saw some evidence of this strategy in my research. Joseph, a level 1 sports student, recognised how dressing in a certain manner can fuel stereotypes, so decided to change his dress pattern so he would fit more easily into college life:

> Joseph: I haven't worn a hood for ... Well, I do the odd time, but not in that way if you know what I mean. I'm trying to change the way I act and the people I hang with.

In terms of Black male youth culture and personal identity issues, such decisions created a conflict for students who believed that to be accepted as serious students they would have to sacrifice part of their identity. Such perceptions echo the findings of Rhamie and Hallam in which Black students recognised 'the negative stereotyped perceptions that White society often had of them' (2002:159) and deliberately opted to adopt the accepted norms of White mainstream culture. Although the Black students in my study did not suggest they were instructed to adopt specified cultural norms, there was a perception amongst the group that some dress codes and behaviour associated with Black culture were not welcome in the college. Consequently students had to decide whether 'to try and cross cultural boundaries' (Fordham and Ogbu, 1986:182), and risk opposition and derision from their Black peers or to try and 'act White' (*ibid*).

Although conforming to school norms in this way may have brought the students some degree of academic success, it was the position most likely attract censure from their Black peers. There is a particular problem for boys who appear incapable of uniting pro-school attitudes with being Black, and instead link 'academic achievement with being gay or effeminate' (Sewell, 2004:107). Accommodating perceived White norms in this way affects personal relationships with sections of the Black community and requires forging new friendship groups. Joseph explained how he managed this situation:

> Joseph: Well, a lot of people think I've changed. They think I'm becoming a pretty boy and all this stuff, but I'm not really bothered, to tell you the truth. But a lot of my friends respect me because I'm sticking at college and stuff. They just think that I'm turning into a goody-goody, but I'm not really bothered

> SP: That's a pretty big sacrifice, leaving your friends and your past behind

> Joseph: Well they went their way, I went my way. They chose, to me, the wrong path and I've gone the right way. That's what keeps my head up.

Accommodation can be perceived as the sell-out position, where individuals adopt the behaviour and practices of the oppressing majority for the sake of their own academic achievement. Although this strategy may produce advantages for individual students, the gains to the Black community appear tenuous and are certainly deferred. However, such accommodation facilitates open access to mainstream systems and affords opportunities for dialogue between Black students and organisational structures.

Covert accommodators

There are Black students who try and become invisible to survive education, adopting a passive, raceless persona so they might focus on their own academic achievement and meet the demands of teachers (Fordham, 1996). Covert accommodators do not actively resist or challenge authority and do not fight back against the domination of an unjust system. Students in this category students wish to get on quietly and as far as possible to be anonymous. This presentation can also be described as selling out, although there is less obvious compromise of personal integrity and Black identity than the overt accommodators. Black students choosing this strategy may be more able to avoid the criticisms of their peers while at the same time gaining favour with their tutors.

Resistors

Academic agitators

Being an academic agitator involves fighting back and consequently maintaining a high degree of racial congruence and gaining the approval of their Black peers. Academically able Black students who use this strategy publically challenge structures or question authority through accepted channels such as student councils or student petitions, using conventional language and presentation.

Educationally this is a high risk strategy for able students as they might be moved from high performing groups to lower level classes, on the grounds that overt challenge is inappropriate in an academic environment and hinders the progress of other students in the group. Although this may result in being re-united with their peer group, as Black students are often over-represented in lower groups, they would deny themselves the opportunity of higher academic achievement. This strategy differs from rude-boy or 'cool-pose' because of its intelligence and lack of bullish aggression and is much more difficult for institutions to manage.

Guerrillas

This final resistance strategy is the 'most enlightening yet difficult to enact' (Noguera, 2003:447). The Black students exercise their resistance through their work. Although they oppose the opinions and views of the teachers they express their disagreement in their written feedback, recognising they would be 'penalised for doing so' (*ibid*:444) in a classroom situation. However, by taking this more subtle option, Black students ensure that they remain in classes for more able students and allow themselves the chance to do well academically. The principal difficulty with this strategy is that by remaining in higher level classes, the students can find themselves removed from the immediate support of their Black peers and as they may appear to be conforming to mainstream culture, they still run the risk of attracting criticism from other Black students. However, by not compromising and challenging authority, the strategy allows individuals to maintain a high degree of racial congruence and personal integrity.

To sum up – Black male students are judged on the way they present themselves in education. Notwithstanding the significant influence of the dominant hegemony, they still have control over which presentation they adopt. Their choices are not fixed and they can move between various strategies at different times in their education journey. Black students will have already made choices over their approaches to secondary education. When transferring to FE they may decide to re-consider or, if this is the first time they have actively thought about their presentation, choose which education strategy they will adopt.

When it comes to such choices, FE colleges have a distinct advantage over schools. For students who have had a difficult secondary school career FE provides the opportunity for a new start. It helps that FE colleges were established to meet the needs of an adult population and some of the irksome rules they resented at schools no longer pertain. There are no uniforms, no bells and no imposed deference. The ethos of FE is wholly consistent with 'cool pose' in its relaxation of formality. Black males find when they enter college that they no longer need to adopt the passive or active resistance strategies they employed at school. Their dress choice, speech patterns and demeanour are no longer challenged in the same way. As two level 2 art students who took part in this research observed, it was possible to:

> Stephen: Just be yourself. You're just being how you are. Your own environment really

> Curtis: It's freedom really

How race influences learning and participation: the college/school experience

Many students who had experienced a difficult journey through secondary education reported that they actually enjoyed college life and found it completely different from school. The 'fresh start, new chance' (Green and Lucas, 2000) ideology of FE became their reality and they felt strongly that their experience of college contrasted sharply to their life in school. Some students believed they had experienced racist treatment by teachers at their school and although such indeterminate, covert racism was difficult to specify, they had been left with a feeling that they were on the receiving end of hostile treatment because of their race. This came out clearly in conversation with Gary and Joseph:

> Gary: I felt let down by school, definitely. I feel like I wasn't treated like the rest at all when I was there. My mum used to say that 'I know it's bad, but you gotta realise that you're the only mixed race, Black student out of all your friends, and you're bigger than everyone else, so you're gonna stand out'.

> (A level student)

> SP: Do you think in anyway they (the college staff) treat you differently because of your ethnicity?

Joseph: No. No I don't. I did find that at my old school, but coming here to where they treat you a lot different. No, not at all. I haven't had no like, kind of, hints or anything like that since I've been here, which I'm quite happy about, 'Cause coming from my last school there was a lot of 'unfair treatment' shall I say.

(Level 1 sports student)

The belief that school teachers treated Black students unfairly because of their ethnicity was constantly stressed by the participants in my inquiry. Damaging 'racial stereotypes of Black people as 'uneducated' and 'under-achievers' ' (Maylor *et al*, 2006:63) still persist in education and Black students continue to be unfairly discriminated against by some teachers. When considered in the context of Ofsted's findings that, although most secondary schools have equal opportunities, multicultural and antiracist policies it was 'rare to find clear procedures for monitoring their implementation' (Ofsted, 1999:13) Gary's and Joseph's comments are not surprising. In this destructive climate Ofsted also found 'racial taunting (was) widespread and a regular fact of life for many minority ethnic pupils' (1999:13). Consequently, for many Black students without rigorous implementation strategies, equal opportunities policies had become paper documents with little or no real meaning.

In contrast, on entering college students had a real opportunity to put secondary school behind them when they went to college. Rather than having to constantly defend themselves, they could concentrate on their studies and academic interests. But although college life appeared to be a significantly better than schools, 'racist name-calling, harassment and stereotyping' (Commission for Black Staff in FE, 2002:62) was commonplace in some colleges and 'many colleges had no effective polices or planned training in this area' (*ibid*). While the Black students who took part in my study believed they were treated better in FE, this was in spite of rather than because of, any planned, strategic management of race relations. In the colleges involved, the staff attitudes were supportive towards Black students, even without dedicated training.

In addition to the perceived generally racist atmosphere of secondary schools, Black students reported unfavourable treatment from staff and said that aggression and humiliation prevailed. Although this was not always necessarily linked to race, students like Gary expressed a belief that their high profile and visibility in schools put them in a position where they could almost inevitably expect such treatment. When asked to describe how college tutors worked with learners in comparison to school teachers, Curtis and Issac replied:

Curtis: They treat you more like adults and less like a kid, even though you are a kid. They've got more respect for you as a person, rather than ... I don't know it's just different. They're not as cheeky either as teachers.

(Level 2 art student)

Issac: They treat you more adultish. They don't shout in your face when you're wrong.

SP: What do they do when you're wrong?

Issac: Just put you right or tell you. Take you to one side and talk to you, instead of trying to make a scene in front of everyone. That's what is seemed like at school. They'd try to make a show of you.

(Level 2 business student)

Black students believed making 'a show' was a common mechanism for controlling students and that school teachers selected individuals to make an example of and demonstrate how insubordination was dealt with. Their use of the word 'cheeky' requires explanation: for this group of students it did not mean loveable or roguish but is the same 'cheeky' referred to by Keith in Eggleston's research (1986, see Chapter 3). It signified an over familiarity by school staff, bordering on dismissiveness. The views and opinions of Black students were not valued or taken seriously. In this sense, 'cheeky' was not a term of endearment: it described staff overstepping professional work boundaries in the ways they spoke to and related with students. This hostility was succinctly summarised by one level 1 sports student:

Peter: In school they just treat you like ... Talk to you like shit.

Black students felt that college tutors demonstrated care beyond perfunctory requirements, almost to the point of treating students as members of a wider extended family, and was a key difference between life at college and life in school. Black students believed they were valued and felt staff actually cared about them, so the potential threat of being treated in a dismissive manner was minimised or completely removed. While at school, students felt they had no option but to tolerate such negative and dismissive staff attitudes. The move to college, however, signalled a change in students' acceptance of such behaviour and they were clear that they would not allow themselves to be treated in such a manner, now that they considered themselves young adults. Students had a clear sense of their self-worth and were certain about their value as individuals. A level 2 business student reflected:

> Moses: The way you get talked to at school, I don't think I'd allow it now. A teacher here couldn't talk to me how I used to get spoken to at school. Teachers used to speak down to you and stuff.

The negative treatment routinely meted out by staff in schools contrasted sharply with their treatment in college. Students felt that college staff actively worked to promote equality and parity among all student groups, as one of the level 1 sports students explained:

> Joseph: They treat you, they treat everyone as equal. Full stop. That's what I think.
>
> SP: And how does that compare with school?
>
> Joseph: A lot different. I found a lot of not, yeah, I could say racism when I was going through school. Like it was race all the time. But when you came to college you don't get any of that.

The way Joseph uses 'equal' here requires explanation. Within a dominant White culture treating 'everyone as equal' can be interpreted as treating everyone as White. However, equal here is about according equal worth to all students. Students were not so naive as to believe that staff were colour-blind, rather equality ensured their difference was recognised and catered for. As such staff at college were perceived in a different light by Black students who viewed staff to be both for the students and like the students, as these students explained:

> John: The way the teachers carry on is completely different to school. The teachers are more like us in a way.
>
> Andrew: They talk to you normal. You are the same as everyone else. There's nothing different about you other than skin tone.
>
> John: And they treat you like equals. And we call the teachers by first names and that's one thing that helps.
>
> Andrew: It's about respect.
>
> John: It's not as if I'm calling him 'Sir' or 'Mr This, Mr That'.
>
> Peter: They're in a higher place.
>
> John: My tutor is fair with everyone. She doesn't discriminate or make it unfair on Black or White people.
>
> Peter: It's more equal here.

John: Even Laura (the course tutor) told us not to look up to her. She's got respect for us and she's on the same level as us. All of the staff are fair. They're firm, but fair.

(Level 1 sports students)

Austin: The teachers at school are different to the teachers at college as well.

Moses: Teachers at school will shout at you.

Austin: They don't really seem to want to help. They don't really seem to care. Teachers at college, they care. But teachers at school just let you do what you want, and they don't try and motivate you.

(Level 2 business students)

Words that were used repeatedly by students were: 'equal', 'respect' and 'care'. These three words encapsulated their view of college. College signalled a new beginning for them. A beginning in which, now confident of their own self worth and with the threat of humiliation and hostility apparently removed, they could engage with learning in a meaningful fashion, and could (for the first time for some of them) begin to take advantage of the potential benefits afforded through education.

Although the Black men and boys who took part in this research project were positive about the staff/student relationships at college, research completed by the *Commission for Black Staff in FE* suggested that this is not the case for all Black students studying in FE:

> African-Caribbean and Asian boys were most likely to be typecast as aggressive or confrontational. This was highlighted by the evidence of a group of Black learners who spoke eloquently of the 'rude and disrespectful' behaviour of some security guards and the negative perceptions of some staff. (*Commission for Black Staff in Further Education*, 2002:55)

Some students who participated in the Commission's report stated that 'the teaching and support they received was less than effective due to tutors' low expectations' (*ibid*) of Black students and unfortunately, unlike the students in my inquiry, not all enjoyed a positive FE experience.

Another key difference between college and school was the expectation that once students were at college they should, and would, take responsibility for managing their own behaviour. College staff made it clear that they did not see themselves in a policing role and that students should of their own accord adopt acceptable practices and behaviours while in college and conform to college rules and regulations. However, as these were 'like standard life rules' (see Michael, in Chapter 3) most students were able to meet this demand. A default outcome of this practice was that students did not feel that they were harassed or chased by staff in the way they had experienced at school. Two of the respondents summed it up:

> Abraham: At the school I went to they were horrible. Well like they weren't horrible but it was like some teacher on your back every day, and it was like that over and again. And they just get you more stressed and it makes you less want to do the work and less want to be in school. So ... Now you're at college it's more up to you innit? So you feel more responsibility on your own half, and you don't get spoon-fed, nothing really. So it's more independent.

> (A level student)

> Curtis: Where it's different from school is like no-one is monitoring. I mean they are monitoring, but if you don't come to your lessons, you don't come to your lessons. It's your choice to do what you want to do.

> (Level 2 art student)

This new responsibility was accepted positively as a difference in the way in which the two sectors operated and was recognised as an endorsement of their adult status and maturity. While the Black students who engaged in this research described better staff relations at college than those they experienced at school, Ofsted have reported that in some secondary school teachers 'were approachable and would give them (the students) a fair hearing if things went wrong' (Ofsted, 2002:14). However, the students involved in my research had not been so fortunate in their schools.

One of the most telling divisions between school and college was the goodwill and humour that characterised college life. At school students expressed a view that academic work and enjoyment were mutually exclusive categories, perhaps reflecting a more traditional view that 'it was considered unscholarly to use humour as a teaching strategy' (Korobkin, 1988:154) and some of the group felt they needed to choose between one or the other, often to the detriment of their academic studies. This dichotomy was not experienced at college and students felt they could comfortably, and confidently, accommodate both humour and study. College tutors and the college curriculum did not force students into to same choice of work or play, but sought to unite the two features together in a symbiotic relationship, as shown by two different groups of sports and art students:

> Joseph: You can have fun here. It's not like a joke, like at school.

Clark: That's the thing. At school you choose either to have a laugh or work. At college you have a laugh and work.

Joseph: You know what I mean.

SP: Why do you have a laugh and work here? Why didn't you have a laugh and work at school?

Joseph: It wasn't like that. It's one or the other man.

(Level 1 sports students)

Angus: Joke in school was someone busting a joke and everyone laughing. Joke here is the teacher joining in a lickle bit, the students all laughing, then it calms down again.

Curtis: You don't carry on how you was in school in college 'cause you'll get nowhere. That's when you're younger. You leave that behind you.

Angus: It's 'cause frequently we have joke here, so no-one gets too hyper, 'cause they know it's alright.

(Level 2 art students)

In college, humour was used positively to encourage students to work, 'to enhance the learning environment' (Garner, 2006:179) and to 'lower tension, boost student morale and increase student attentiveness' (Torok, McMorris and Lin, 2004:18) by harnessing the positive, productive benefits of humour. Interestingly, unlike the conformists in Sewell's 2004 study, students did not feel that they had to break rank with their peers and humour helped them to 'embrace both the values of school and of their own Black peer group' (*ibid*: 104).

In this section I have described the different ways race has influenced learning for Black students in the FE and school sectors. After feeling let down by their schools, the students found that colleges provided a more satisfying learning environment. These differences were real, apparent and *felt*. However, according to other research (see *Report of the Commission for Black Staff in FE*, 2002) not all Black students in all colleges have enjoyed a positive learning experience in FE.

Racism in schools, FE and wider society

All the Black students who participated in my study were critically aware of race, how it impacted on them and how it influenced the chances they had in society. For them race acted as 'a filter through which they interpreted the world' (Ofsted, 2002:15) and most of those interviewed strongly believed that race had played a significant role in their school experience. Some students believed there were some teachers and pupils in their secondary schools who held racist views, so creating tensions between student cohorts of different ethnicities and producing a factionalised student population based on race. This was clearly explained by an A level student who stated that:

> Abraham: At my school there was a lot of racial tensions. In my school a lot of the teachers had like certain ... There were always tensions between Black and mixed race and the Asian students as well. There were always them tensions. And there was a racial bias that the Asian students got. I felt that the Asian students got better treatment than the Black students did.

Although students endured the covert and overt racist attitudes of some teachers and pupils while at school, they did not think that college staff held the same racial biases. These level 2 business students had the following tale to tell about their time in school:

> Moses: That school, it was so far in the countryside that when the Black people came...
>
> Barry: They were intimidated by us.
>
> Moses: So you've got teachers saying 'It will be nice to have a splash of colour' when we was coming.
>
> Barry: Snide remarks like 'You've all been painted with the same brush'.
>
> Moses: They'd say sly things like that. The pupils were like that as well. When we had to do about slavery, all the White kids were laughing, do you get me?
>
> Barry: That's school.

Black students believed that college staff worked hard to ensure parity of treatment across *all* student populations and students were not selected out or treated unfavourably because of their ethnicity. Abraham and Peter clarified this position in the following way:

> Peter: In my old school you used to get picked on because of your race all the time. You did this because you're Black and all that. But here you don't get that.
>
> (Level 1 sports student)
>
> Abraham: Now I'm at college there's not them biases. All I've got to compare to is school where there was very strong racial bias. Now I'm at college it don't really matter as much but it was a big part of when I was in school.
>
> (A level student)

Although Black students thought the college staff were not racist, they did not believe this to be true of all the students. They thought some of their peers harboured racist beliefs and attitudes which were openly expressed on occasion,. This was described by these level 2 art students:

> Curtis: Before they know they put you into one group, one column quickly, before they even know what they're talking about, before they even know you.
>
> Stephen: It's like they're quick to stereotype.
>
> Curtis: Yeah, stereotype. It's like because he's Black or something, he's gonna be like that.
>
> Stephen: Exactly.
>
> SP: So is that students or is that staff?
>
> Curtis: That's just students. They shouldn't really say stuff when they don't know what they are talking about.

Some students were prepared to make false allegations about their Black peers, identifying them as perpetrators of acts they did not commit, as these level 2 business students told me:

> Austin: Her purse went missing and rather than asking us if we knew any-thing about it she's gone and started saying it was us.
>
> Moses: She's gone straight to the teacher and said our names.
>
> Austin: And when she's got home at night she's found it. She hasn't come and apologised or nothing.

To protect against the persistence of racist attitudes and behaviour of this kind, many Black students chose their friendship groups on the grounds of race and formed monocultural or all-Black friendship groups, promoting Fordham's notion of 'kinship' (1996:283) and solidarity between Black people.

A further racialised stereotype of Black male students was apparent in the way some White women students avoided forming friendships with 'the big Black boy' (Sewell, 1997:25). Their reasoning appeared to be that some of them per-ceived Black males as over-sexualised. The Black students described their ex-periences thus:

> Clive: Some of the gal are stuck up.
>
> Dwaine: You can't say that.
>
> Clive: Yeah they are. You know they are.
>
> Kevin: It's 'cause they don't want a man.

Clive: They're walking around college, having a laugh, and as soon as you say 'You alright ladies?' they just look at you and carry on walking. You get me?

Paul : They know you want one thing.

Clive: I just want to know her name. There's nothing wrong with that.

(Level 1 sports students)

Moses: That girl's arrogant.

Austin: Who?

Moses: You know, that girl. She thinks she's too nice.

Austin: What gal?

Moses: We always see her man. She's stuck up as well.

(Level 2 business students)

Black students interpreted such avoidance as aloofness and did not appear to appreciate why they would be snubbed in this way, choosing to interpret the women's behaviour as snobbish and class-based. Although there may well have been class-based reasons for this rejection, it is interesting to note that these young men did not identify that the behaviour could have been racialised and they did not appear to recognise that they might have been perceived as threatening or sexually predatory.

Finally, in their assessment of racism in society, the students observed that for a Black person living in the UK the all-pervasive nature of racism made everything harder and more difficult in life. A level 1 sports student summed up the impact of racism in society:

John: What colour you are matters. If you're Black it makes an impact. Life's harder being Black. No matter how hard you put a smile on your face, you're going to have to work extra hard to please somebody. My mum says to me 'As a Black youth in a White society you're going to have to work extra hard'. A White person will put in the same work, but you're going to have to put in double effort to get somewhere in life.

Conclusion

This chapter has shown how the impact of race, as denoted by skin colour, was considered by many of the Black men and boys as an inevitability from which there was no escape and that all Black people could expect life to work against them in their efforts to achieve. Many of the Black students believed the all pervasive nature of racism was so great, that in order to achieve anything at all, they were compelled to make additional effort. Racism did not only routinely hinder Black people's life chances, it also pre-determined them.

Because of the toxic environment in schools Black boys often found themselves trapped in a narrow set of limited presentations: either to become the destructive, aggressive underachiever or to be the subservient, submissive student. Either presentation required them to make some degree of sacrifice and they have been obliged to either give up the opportunity of academic achievement or to surrender their cultural identity. FE, however, which is predicated on catering for the needs of adult learners and which values the contributions students can make to their own learning, has been successful in providing Black boys and men with a less negative learning environment. In FE learners are expected to be active partners in their own learning and to take responsibility for their studies. In this environment, released from damaging assumptions made by some staff in schools which configured Black boys as incapable of achieving, Black boys and men were able to leave tired stereotypes behind and have developed a new educational identity which has both maintained their cultural identity and enabled them to engage positively with education.

6

The significance of support for educational success

Introduction

> In the English lexicon, 'support' refers to aid or assistance or the addition of strength to that which cannot stand on its own. (Lee *et al*, 1999:9)

Because FE colleges provide the greatest range of courses offered in any education establishment ranging from pre-entry qualifications through to degree level programmes, they have attracted the most diverse population of students. As a result of this diversity FE colleges, more than any other education sector, are critically aware of the scope of student support needs and the different types of assistance learners require to enable them to complete their programmes successfully, often while simultaneously performing 'work-roles, carer-roles, leisure-roles' (Jacklin and Le Riche, 2009: 735). Consequently colleges have an acute understanding of 'student support systems [which] have become increasingly important' (Dhillon *et al*, 2008: 282) feature of college life.

Most FE colleges have dedicated student support teams committed to helping students achieve their primary learning target. While these teams 'may have multiple functions' (Lee-Tarver, 2006:525), the principle 'purpose of these teams is to provide educational assistance for students at risk of academic failure' (*ibid*). Colleges have a vested interest in student achievement as they receive funding based on student attainment and they attract future students through their reputations. It is therefore to every college's advantage to do all they can to ensure that students achieve positive outcomes for the courses they have enrolled on and to provide services which will help them to achieve.

This chapter describes the organisation and structure of college based student support teams in relation to the needs of Black men and boys. It considers the significance of ideological positioning and how this has influenced the effectiveness of support. It examines questionable support systems before finally identifying how Black men, without the support of centralised college systems, have engineered and built their own support mechanisms.

The role of college based student support systems

The structure of student support departments varies from organisation to organisation according to its institutional goals and priorities and its student population. Jacklin and Le Riche (2009:735) described student support as a 'socially situated, complex, multifaceted' service which has been organised to satisfy local need and to fulfil legal obligations. However, regardless of the individual and the particular circumstances of each organisation, each must comply with legislation and advice issued by the Department for Education (DfE) in 2010. As a minimum, each college is obliged to:

- eliminate discrimination and other conduct prohibited by the Equality Act 2010
- advance equality of opportunity between people who share a protected characteristic and people who do not share it
- foster good relations across all characteristics between people who share a protected characteristic and people who do not share it. (DfE, 2010:21)

The aim of the 2010 Equality Act regarding colleges was to ensure they developed systems which met the needs of all minority populations and that all college users learned to work together in a mutually respectful environment characterised by a spirit of collegiality.

In addition to meeting these requirements, colleges were also obliged to set

> equality objectives that best suit their individual circumstances and contribute to the welfare of their pupils and the school community. Objectives are not intended to be a 'tick box' exercise, but they do need to be specific and measurable. (*ibid*:25)

This is a significant statement. It compels colleges to engage with a meaningful and substantive equality implementation strategy and discourages them from engaging with perfunctory, superficial, quick-fix approaches. Colleges that have invested in student support and have well developed structures in place should not find it onerous to meet this requirement. However, not all colleges have made such an investment and for some organisations achieving this standard will present a significant challenge. These colleges could experience even greater difficulties in meeting the needs of Black and other minority groups who may have distinct and unique support needs.

Rather than being hapless victims, reliant on the whims of a fickle education system which may not be willing or able to try and meet their students' 'academic and emotional support' (Dhillon *et al*, 2008:283) needs and because Black students' needs are 'different from 'mainstream' students' (Rollock *et al*, 1992:243), Black men and boys, have independently developed 'their own networks of support' (Dhillon *et al*, 2008:246) which have enabled them to persist and achieve within FE.

The importance of student support systems

The decision to study at college 'brings with it considerable changes' (Jones *et al*, 1997:26) for all students, some of which students could reasonably predict. However for Black and other ethnic minority students both male and female, 'successful transition involves greater challenges' (Nelson *et al*, 2012: 85). Many students require support to achieve academically at college and such support 'is particularly important' (*ibid*) for students who may, because of cultural differences, lack easy access to traditional college based support mechanisms. It has been found that 'effective provision of support enhanced motivation to learn whilst also assisting in [student] transition' (Gidman *et al*, 2001:352) and that 'students who do not relate emotionally, socially and academically to the institutional culture may withdraw and leave without completing their programme of study' (Dhillon *et al*, 2008:282). For this reason, it is imperative that colleges work to produce effective support systems that meet the needs of all their students of whatever ethnicity and devise strategies that meet the distinctive circumstances and requirements of each group.

Support systems which are most significant in helping students achieve and remain on programme are 'academic, self-development and emotional' (*ibid*: 283). These three systems are mutually dependent and provide the foundation for students to engage effectively with their chosen programme of study and achieve. If students lack support in any one of these areas, it is far more likely, although not inevitable, that they will struggle on their programme and may ultimately be unsuccessful in their studies or leave the programme before completion. Many college student support systems are broadly organised under these three main areas identified by Dhillon (2008). The relationship between each is illustrated in the diagram below:

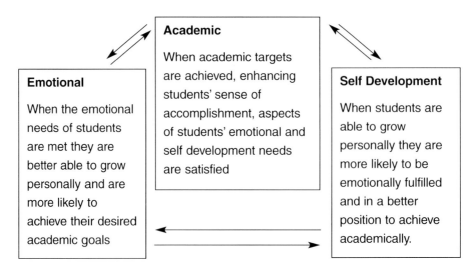

Figure 1: The student support triangle

It is unfortunate that some colleges have struggled to meet key aspects of their ethnic minority students' personal, social and cultural needs. Because self and emotional development are linked to educational achievement, these colleges have also failed to meet the academic needs of these groups effectively.

It is also important to consider the ideological positioning of college support systems, as these philosophies have influenced and continue to affect the manner in which support is provided in colleges. These ideologies may be divided into five broad categories:

> Pastoral (drawing on the metaphor of a shepherd caring for their flock, especially the weak), social democratic (caring for the vulnerable pushed aside in a capitalist society), patriarchal (caring for disadvantaged inferiors) ... community (which involves self-help and peer support) and business (which concerns the student as customer). (Jacklin and Le Riche, 2009:737)

For Black students it is vital that an appropriate ideological position is adopted, one which values and respects Black learners as individuals; recognises the challenging historical and contemporary influences of race and racism on Black communities and individuals; and takes account of the influence of race on learning. However well intended, pastoral, social democratic and patriarchal ideologies, with their suggestions of hierarchies, latent bigotries and potentially racist attitudes, cannot effectively meet the needs of Black students. The fourth model, the community model, which recognises the contribution of the Black community in identifying and meeting its own needs, putting the students' needs before institutional needs, is far more likely to be well received by Black students. The fifth and final model, the business model, although considering the needs of Black students from a customer perspective, still predominantly places the organisation at the forefront and therefore its relevance for Black students is questionable.

Whether through formal college systems or by other means, learner support is a vital component of success for all learners. Students who can access and use support are 'more likely to achieve' (Petty, 2004:513) than those who do not. Within the context of educational exclusion and marginalisation, relevant, useful support is even more important for Black men and boys. Sadly, 'students who have individual needs arising from ... social or cultural difference' (Gutteridge, 2001:2) may be viewed as too 'costly to support because they tend not to fit easily into a system designed' for the White majority (*ibid*). The challenge for colleges is how they will achieve an acceptable ideology and what sorts of assistance they will provide to Black students to support them to engage effectively with education.

Questionable support systems

While helpful peers and other agencies are essential for achieving in college, not all support is useful in promoting academic attainment. Education-antagonistic students who have abandoned 'both the means and the goals of schooling' (Sewell, 1997:116) can quickly undermine the relevance and value of learning. They become 'disgruntled and eventually disillusioned' (Connor, 2003:127) about the possibilities of education and instead have chose to 'reject the world of schooling' (Sewell, 1997:118). While these learners may have achieved social high status and are 'considered cool' (Connor, 2003:31) by their peers because they have rejected the legitimacy of study, they fail to make academic progress. What is more, they are able to persuade other students to reject learning and education because of their high status. Rather than being an aid to learning, peers then become a negative influence on academic achievement.

Some education-resistant students have taken to 'just idly walking the streets' (Centre for Social Justice, 2009:79), opting to sell 'drugs and be part of a gang' culture which offers young people a different 'version of mainstream social climbing' (*ibid*). While gang culture may not pose a significant threat to students when they are actually inside college buildings, gangs act as a constant reminder of an 'alternative lifestyle' (Sewell, 1997:118) and an economy which appears to offer sizeable financial rewards. Unfortunately not all young Black men are able to resist the allure of 'quick money' (*ibid*) and will choose the opportunity to become part of a gang for the immediate benefits it can offer in preference to studying at college and its potential deferred gains.

Black men and boys who have been unable to access relevant helpful community or other support systems, may be obliged to utilise centralised college support systems. While the intention of these systems is to provide useful support, they have often been constructed from a dominant White perspective and therefore have frequently excluded Black students through either 'overt racism' (Anderson, 2010:4) or 'subtle prejudice' (*ibid*:6) which is expressed through colour blindness. Colour-blindness 'functions to erase differences among people and it forces those who differ from the White norm to assimilate into or to imitate Whiteness'(*ibid*:260). Although colour-blindness may position itself as a kind of benevolent care 'the polite language of race' (Mirza, 2009: 45), it is racist because it fails to recognise and accommodate the *differing* needs of *different* groups and to acknowledge that diversity demands a range of responses. The colour blindness adopted as an easy, non-confrontational option by some institutions fails as a strategy through its apathy, 'its well-meaning false optimism' (*ibid*). Framed in this way, colour blindness reveals itself as no more than a lame excuse used by those who would wish to 'ignore the realities of racism and social divisions'. Colour-blindness is dangerous because it refuses to 'challenge racism' (Mirza, 2009:45), and without challenge, developing individualised support for different groups becomes impossible.

Support in transition to college

The 'positive adjustment of Black students to life on predominantly White campuses' (Rollock *et al*, 1992:243) continues to raise questions for Black students and for academic and support staff in colleges and schools alike. Within the UK, most FE campuses could be accurately described as predominantly White institutions. Because some Black students, due to repeatedly negative experiences, have developed a general inclination 'to mistrust Whites' (Phelps *et al*, 2001:209), successful adjustment to college life after a potentially damaging school experience becomes even more vital.

As a consequence of being denied educational opportunity in other environments and in order to facilitate transition to college life, Black men and boys have created their own support mechanisms. In common with other marginalised groups, there have been no ready-made templates to assist Black men and boys in this endeavour and they have made or improvised their own solutions. This has relied heavily on the African oral history tradition of verbally passing on useful information to others in their community.

A cornerstone of this support has been the concept of 'fictive kinship' (Fordham, 1996:283). In Fordham's construction, Black people identify all other Black people as potential allies, willing to give help to and accept help from any other Black person. The notion of fictive kinship has allowed Black people to quickly establish contact with one another and to make requests of each other which would be expected to be agreed, in much the same way that biological family members would. The benefits of this approach are that Black students are enabled to contact an extended network far beyond their family relations and personal friends, some of whom could be reasonably expected to have the skills or knowledge needed for a particular situation. Access to this network is not dependent on money and so recognises the difficult financial situation many students find themselves in. The relationship is based instead on an unspoken reciprocal agreement that at some unspecified time in the future, support will be returned to the individual or community that originally provided the assistance. In this way local knowledge and other resources are shared between members of the Black community for the benefit of the whole community. In an extension of this logic, the arrival of a Black college principal, who would be expected by other members of the Black community to have some knowledge of the societal and academic challenges facing Black people studying in the UK, may precipitate an increase in the number of Black students attending a particular establishment.

Community histories are also important in this regard and colleges, often initially as a result of proximity to residential areas where Black people live, and later by reputation, may become known as a good place for Black people to study. Black men and boys will share information about their experiences at particular colleges with other Black people through their personal networks such as part-time employment, music venues, church attendance or sports clubs. In this way a college's positive reputation will become common knowledge. By the same token, negative experiences will also be shared and may dissuade Black students from attending certain colleges.

In common with other sections in society, advances in technology have extended the ways in which Black men and boys communicate with and support each other. Social networking sites have enabled Black people to stay in contact with one another when they are away from campus and to share essential information. Black students no longer need to wait until the next time they are in college to check information and they can clarify points quickly and easily with each other. Further, mobile technology has allowed Black students to contact one another while in transit, so they can share helpful information regarding equipment they need to take to college, or let one another know about a teaching room or tutor change.

Black students have also been able to set up informal support groups among themselves. While such groups may not be able to satisfy the entire academic, self-development and emotional needs of each group member, they are a readily available form of support and, critically, the Black men themselves have full authority to set group agendas and steer the group's direction. The informality of the group enables it to be made and remade at any time depending on the level of need.

Conclusion

Student success is a fundamental goal of all colleges. Effective student support systems can have 'a positive impact on student outcomes' (Nelson *et al*, 2012:94) and help to achieve the goal of academic success. However, securing academic success and overcoming 'initial educational disadvantage' is a challenge which requires 'the right combination of instruction, study and a supportive environment' (Muraskin, 1997:20). In a constantly changing climate with the ever increasing need to enhance student success rates, colleges 'have an obligation to provide the necessary mileau to support students to engage academically, socially and personally' (Nelson *et al*, 2012:84). This is important for all students. An appropriate centralised college support infrastructure is even more necessary for students who may be 'at risk of disengaging from their learning' (*ibid*:94), such as Black and ethnic minority students or students who have had previous poor educational experiences. In this respect positive 'intervention assistance for students at risk should be the primary task for student support teams' (Lee-Tarver, 2006:531). Within this context, colleges need to critically examine the range of services provided to Black and ethnic minority students to determine if they are adequately meeting these students' needs. The need to develop relevant support mechanisms becomes more urgent, as traditionally, 'Black students may not seek these services at rates commensurate with their levels of need or comparable to their White peers' (Rollock *et al*, 1992:243). Colleges have to find ways to engage in a critical dialogue with Black students and the wider Black community so that FE can develop a 'strategic approach to student support ... designed to promote ... the facilities, the atmosphere and attitudes to learning' (Jacklin and Le Riche, 2009:736) needed to secure success and which acknowledges the 'institutional factors and the cultures and contexts within which support operates' (*ibid*:737).

However, it is important to recognise that colleges do not have sole responsibility for meeting the educational needs of Black students and that the 'provision of (college) support facilities cannot guarantee an effective support system' (Dhillon *et al*, 2008:283). For this reason, Black communities must also work to find ways of supporting Black men and boys pursuing their college journeys. This support begins in the home environment because 'families have a major influence on achievement' (Henderson and Mapp, 2002:7) and students are more likely to succeed when there is 'strong support from parents, peers and members of the community' (Lee *et al*, 1999:15). The next chapter considers various support systems available to Black students.

7

How Black men and boys
create support systems

Introduction

While studying at college Black students designed and created their own support mechanisms. These were organised into three main categories: family support, staff support and peer support. This chapter looks at these mechanisms and discusses how effectively each system met the needs of the students in my study.

Students also referred to their own personal motivation and self-determination to succeed which were often accompanied by varying degrees of moral outrage and a deep-seated desire to prove others, often unhelpful or suspected racist school teachers, wrong. It was these feelings which, even in difficult circumstances, enabled Black men and boys to persist within education and continue to strive achieve sought-after qualifications.

Staff Support

The support category students most often referred to by Black men and boys was staff support. Although dedicated student support provision was available in both the colleges, students made little reference to these services and appeared to try to manage whatever issue they were dealing with without recourse to centralised college support systems. When talking of staff support, Black men and boys referred solely to the integrated class based support provided by the main class tutor responsible for teaching the lesson. This integrated student support provided by the regular teacher appeared to be far more acceptable to the Black students, as it did not single them out in a negative way or label them as having particular problems.

This integrated in-class support was low-key in nature and consequently students did not feel they had been identified as either challenging or deficient, needing additional separate assistance. The manner of working chosen by FE tutors was also significant as this same student population had attracted much unwelcome negative staff attention during their school years and, some of the students, had become used to staff attention being synonymous with being in trouble (see Wright, 1998; London Development Agency, 2004). Worse still, other Black students saw it as a way of identifying them as 'as mentally retarded' (Noguera, 2003:432) and needing remedial support.

The two contrasting reasons why students received more attention from staff had one common feature: both were predicated on a deficit model which required corrective intervention. Because of the negative associations of support of this kind, some Black students had become sceptical and suspicious of individualised or specialist staff attention, equating it with punitive or detrimental action or fearing it signalled institutional surveillance. It was significant not one student who took part in this research project identified the specific services of student support as useful or appropriate to their needs, nor did they make any reference to individualised staff support. The elective distancing from formal support systems suggests a common feeling of unease among Black men and boys regarding such support. A level 1 sports student explained why the college counselling service was unnecessary:

> Joseph: Counselling? I've never had to use it. My tutors do enough of that for me. If I need support I go to my tutors or any one of my teachers because I know them well. They've built my life up. They're the main one. They've kept me on board and helped me a lot. If I wasn't coming to this college I wouldn't be doing as well in my life as what I am now. I've got a lot of thanks for them.

The single most important factor which made the support offered by class tutors acceptable and useful to Black students was their belief that college staff genuinely cared about their welfare and could be trusted as expert tutors and professional educators or, as several remarked, simply as 'friends' who wanted to make a positive difference to their future. Although this view represented an affirmative recognition of tutor support, it also raised challenges for Black students, who could potentially feel betrayed if at some later time they were reprimanded by the same tutors. If this happened it could become even more difficult for Black students to work with or trust these tutors afterwards. Trevor and Clement explained the positive nature of staff/student relations:

Trevor: They treat you as friends. They can trust you, and we can trust them.

(Level 2 sports student)

Clement: If I needed help I wouldn't be struggling, I've got teachers who I like to think are friends who would help me.

(A level student)

Two of the A level students were sufficiently perceptive to recognise that there might be professional boundaries that constrained the teaching staff. So while they appreciated the mutual respect that existed between staff and students, they viewed college tutors primarily as professional educators, tasked with teaching students:

Abraham: You feel like they're here to teach you, you're here to learn. It's got that mutual respect.

Gary: They know that you are here to learn; they know you are a person. It's kinda like friendship but there's a boundary you don't cross. You don't step it and they don't come in. I believe if you act normal and give them respect, the same comes back to you. It's a mutual respect thing.

Abraham: They think we're mature as well

These students' perception of college tutors as friends was for them a crucial difference between school and college. They had not seen their school-teachers as friends and were deeply distrustful of them. They believed that student confidentiality would not be protected by school teachers but that they would share student information with other staff without hesitation:

Trevor: In school you couldn't trust them, 'cause if you told them something I know they would go and tell the headmaster or something. And they treated you as little kids as well. In college they treat you as adults.

(Level 2 sports student)

College staff were seen as making a reciprocal, personal and emotional investment in the students. Indeed, some Black students felt the level of investment from staff was so great that it went beyond friendship and was more akin to the relationship of a concerned family member who was genuinely interested in each student's welfare. Two level 1 sports students described this relationship in the following way:

Lawrence: They've got this emotion for you. It's like Lewis, he treats you like a brother, like 'I want you to do well', and he's proper preaching to you like my Dad or something. They don't speak to you aggressively, like nastily.

Clark: It's just getting a point across.

Joseph: I wouldn't say they speak to me aggressively. It's only like when they're trying to show me something.

The irritation that is sometimes apparent in close family relationships was revealed in this remark. Lewis (a Black college tutor) is described as a 'brother' who 'preaches' like a 'Dad'. Yet in his desire for students to do well Lewis is still *preaching* to the students. Significantly though, Lewis' behaviour was tolerated by the Black men and boys, who were prepared to suspend any resistance they might feel towards authority if that authority was displayed by tutors who the Black students believed genuinely cared about them. This perception further supported the claim made by some students that college was more like home to them, which had effectively become populated by surrogate family members. Joseph, a level 1 sports student, described the relationship in more depth in the following way:

Joseph: The college done well to keep me here and keep me in a straight line, 'cause at times I was going off track. But like I said, because of the respect the college had for me and they wanted to get me somewhere, they stuck at it and I'm still here now.

The college tutors' closeness to and acceptance of Black students was demonstrated in the familiar way staff chose to communicate with students and how they dressed and presented themselves. As a result, while acknowledging the different roles held by staff and learners, Black students were willing to view college staff more as friends and considered them to be operating on the same level as themselves. This more casual approach directly contrasted with their school experience, which had been characterised by rigid hierarchies and formalities. These level 1 sports students described their relationship with staff like this:

John: I think most students see college teachers more as a friend than a teacher. Because (our) teachers don't dress in a shirt and tie. My teacher dresses in tracksuit bottoms and trainers, and when I look at her I don't see her really as a teacher I see her more as a friend who's trying to help me get somewhere. I think if other students see teachers the same way I do and it's a nice friendly environment. But if Laura (the course tutor) was in a suit and tie and told me to call her 'Miss' I'd look at her and maybe think we're not going to get along. It's like I have to look up to you if I'm calling you Miss.

Clark: What teachers we got they're on a level aren't they? On our level anyway. We get along.

Abraham, who was studying A levels added:

> Abraham: At school you still call the teacher 'Miss'. At school it's 'Miss Jones' or 'Miss' or whatever. At college it's calling them by their first names. You get to know the teachers, that's why you connect with them more on a personal level.

Although the staff adopted an informal and relaxed approach in working with and supporting students, they maintained an appropriate balance between demonstrating concern and not overstepping personal boundaries by becoming too familiar or prying into students' private lives. Clearly distinguishing between providing support and managing students' perceptions of them as surrogate family members was a constant occupational difficulty for the tutors as they knew they might need to take action which could appear contrary to the act of a friend or concerned relative. When discussing how college tutors managed discussions on personal issues, the students reported that staff handled these situations professionally and sensitively:

> Angus: I know that basically you can talk to anyone in college. We have one-to-one stuff and they ask 'How's college?' 'How's work?'

> Curtis: Mine talks about other stuff. Stuff outside. She opens a discussion about the weekend and stuff, anything in the news. Anything that's gone on really.

> SP: Does that feel comfortable or does it feel she's too nosy?

> Curtis: It feels comfortable. It don't feel nosy ' cause she's getting it off the news. So it's good cause she knows what's happening around us. And she talks about our age group and our race, how it's vulnerable out on the streets and stuff. She just tells you to keep a cool head. She gives good advice.

> (Level 2 art students)

> Issac: I've had a couple of problems at home and what not and I can talk to the teachers here. They can understand and advise me. They try and get me on the right path, speak to the right people I've got to speak to. It's a lot more helpful.

> (Level 2 business student)

These comments were particularly significant. Here was a college tutor willing to acknowledge the difficulty of life 'out on the streets', issues of race and youth culture. She showed an awareness 'of the complex identities of the boys, in a context where racism worked on a number of levels' (Sewell, 2004:

103) and demonstrated empathy with the problems that can be experienced when trying to navigate what Issac calls 'the right path'.

However, although the college tutors were viewed as approachable and supportive, most were White. So the students still took the view that better support could be achieved if there were more Black staff, indicating the extension of the idea of 'fictive kinship'. The contribution of Black staff in teaching Black students is explored in detail in Chapter 8.

College staff were seen to be wanting students to achieve and do well on their programmes and were prepared to invest in Black students so that they could achieve their full potential. In contrast to school teachers, college tutors were viewed as being encouraging and motivating. This view was succinctly expressed by Curtis, Angus and Stephen, who were studying art courses at level 2.

> Stephen: I don't think they underestimate anyone. I think staff know what you're capable of. They know you can do the work.
>
> Curtis: They believe in your abilities.
>
> Angus: Yeah, always. They always like encourage you. They know you can do it.

Similar views were expressed by Gary, an A level student and Gregory and Joseph who were on a level 1 sports course:

> Gary: If all you need is that little something to turn you on, they will try to help you. At school they thought you weren't bothered or you were lazy so they thought there was no point. Here, they'll try and help you. They don't spoon feed you but if you need help, and if you want to be helped, they'll help you.
>
> Gregory: They always give me a chance.
>
> Joseph: They want us to join in. They want us to be taking part.

While tutors were viewed as supportive, they were not considered to be foolish or naive or to be unaware about the students who were not committed to their studies. When discussing absence from college these two A level students observed:

> Abraham: Another thing I like about college, is the teachers, you know. I've had four colds in the last three weeks and I've told the teachers and they've been 'Like, fine'. When I was at school they were like 'Don't catch a cold'.
>
> Gary: There wasn't much trust there. Here, teachers know when you're pulling a fast one, but generally they do trust you.

Levi and Joseph summarised tutor support in the following way:

> Joseph: My teacher said to me I'd by signing on by the age of 19. That's what he said to me. I can't wait to see him. I just can't wait to see him. I just want to take my booklet of qualifications and say to him 'This is no thanks to you'. That's what I want to say

> (Level 1 sports student)

> Levi: The best thing about college is teachers. I can talk to them

> (Entry level student)

Peer support systems

In the absence of cultural support from the college, students formed their own informal support groups. They expressed a strong inclination to associate with other Black students both academically and socially. This in itself appeared to be a supportive mechanism as it gave the students a positive sense of self and a feeling of security as an ethnic minority community within the college. This sentiment was expressed in vivid terms by these level 1 sports students:

> John: The people we move with, care for each other. I care for my own, as simple as that.

> Peter: Dog eat dog.

> John: I care for you niggers.

> Peter: Black people. They're the main people I hang around with.

John demonstrated his strong endorsement of the notion of 'fictive kinship'. He saw being Black as the defining feature of his own identity even though this same identity was 'stigmatised by the dominant society' (Fordham, 1996: 283) in which a 'dog eat dog' mentality persisted. In the absence of other relevant college based support systems to sanction the positive worth of being a Black minority, peer affirmation by other Black students was viewed as a vital tool in maintaining Black cultural pride and integrity.

Black men and boys believed they could communicate more effectively with students who had the same racial identity and a similar understanding of the issues associated with race. Thus, even though the group were diverse and very different from each other in a variety of ways including, for example, age, employment status or family construction, they felt confident that they shared a common core understanding based on having experienced similar situations during their development. The group were certain this assumed commonality of experience was capable of promoting better communication between them.

At the same time this positioning raised an interesting ambiguity for the students engaged with my inquiry: on one level they were keen to identify their own personalised style and individualism, while they were also keen to support the notion of a collective identity. However when expressed by those in authority, for example school teachers, this same collectivism was not accepted and students resisted being subsumed into a homogenous 'African-Caribbean subculture' where all students were seen as identical (Sewell, 1997: 44). This apparent contradiction in perception highlighted the complex issues of identity formation and personal presentation. A level 1 sports student explained his feelings towards other Black students in the following way:

> John: Most of the time Black people get more at the same level, because you've got the same issues and things.
>
> SP: What issues?
>
> John: Not issues, but the same things about you.

In this exchange John draws attention to the solidarity that existed among Black men and boys as self-supported learners. In doing so he inadvertently presented a powerful alternative to the idea of role models and mentoring. While John, like Sewell (1997), acknowledged Black staff could have a useful role in supporting Black students as they navigated FE, in the absence of such role models these students had, without the direction, support or encouragement of centralised college systems, successfully produced their own support mechanisms which enabled them to persist and achieve within the FE environment. This idea is returned to in Chapter 8.

Black students considered it important to have strong, reliable friendship groups while studying in college: groups who could offer emotional support and support against potential aggressors, if needed. Association with Black peers was viewed as a kind of insurance policy to protect against potential or actual violence. In some ways Black students operated a siege mentality and prepared for and expected the worst as a matter of course. Consequently in exchanges 'involving conflict or competition' with other college users including tutors, 'fictive kinship' took on a heightened significance where peers were seen as providing shelter from the storm (Fordham, 1996:72). This view was poignantly illustrated by level 1 sports students John and Tony:

> John: When I stop, think and look around me, that's when I realise the majority of people around me are Black. But I don't have no objection in

hanging round with White people, I just feel more secure with my own people than I would with White people. I don't know why. It's just something I do.

SP: When you're talking about security, what is it that you think Black people would give you, that you're not sure White people would?

John: Defence.

SP: Against what?

John: Anything really. No matter what, I think Black people as a team, we stick together more. If there's a group of Black friends, we will stick together more than a group of White friends.

Tony: If you hang around with Black people they're always there for you. They'll mind my back

John was clear that Black peers were likely to offer each other support in a way that White students could not. The solidarity he perceived existed between Black students was not present in mixed ethnicity groups and he could not rely on support from White peers in the same way. As a result Black students instinctively congregated together to meet a perceived need.

Although the group declared they were comfortable with their mostly White tutors and believed they enjoyed good support from them, they did not see college tutors as the ones to give them emotional support and it was their Black peers who fulfilled this role when needed. Again, it appeared to be the case that formal college student support mechanisms were not relevant to Black students' needs and that friendship groups were better placed to address their concerns. A level 1 sports student told me this:

SP: So how do you get something wrong sorted out? Has anything gone wrong?

Peter: Something has gone wrong. I spoke to my mates and they just helped me through it. It's not like major things, it's like little things. Little things going down in college, they've helped me get through it.

SP: Has that been enough, your mates?

Peter: Yeah, so far. I've never had to go to my tutor about anything yet.

The high level of camaraderie and personal support was so significant among Black men and boys that they were even prepared to take the blame for a peer's actions for the sake of solidarity. The motivation to do so appeared to be an affirmation of 'fictive kinship' where 'Black people are expected to 'stick together' in the face of challenge or difficulties' (Ogbu, 1991:267). Two other level 1 sports students demonstrated how this kinship was enacted both within college and elsewhere:

> Dwaine: I've took your blame. I've took your blame plenty of times.
>
> Clive: But I've took your blame.
>
> Dwaine: There's even times out of college.

In addition to the personal and emotional support they gave each other, Black men and boys also offered each other a good deal of scholarly support. In contrast to emotional support which appeared to be reserved solely for peers who shared the same racial identity, academic support was offered to all peers in a reciprocal relationship where other students, be they Black or White, were willing to offer and receive academic support. In this complex system of monocultural and cross-cultural friendship and support, Black students were adopting the mantle of 'acting White' (Fordham and Ogbu, 1986: 176) in striving for academic excellence, while at the same time enlisting the support of both Black *and* White peers and breaking out of Black-only 'fictive kinship' groups. This seemed to be a form of academic hustling where Black students were willing to 'exploit interpersonal relationships for material and non material benefits' (Ogbu, 1991:265).

Hustling, however, usually means exploiting 'non-conventional resources to tap into the 'street economy' (*ibid*). In this situation Black students were accessing a conventionally valued resource (education) by conventionally accepted means (student self-help groups) and had successfully fused 'activities which [were] perceived as uncool' (Majors and Billson, 1992:46) into a personalised hybrid, which allowed them to persist academically and retain their credibility among their Black peer group, while also achieving high levels of academic success. In this instance Black students did not appear to be different from their White counterparts who were also trying to achieve academically. This collaborative peer support was explained by Gary and Abraham, who were studying A levels, and Joseph and Clark, who were completing sports programmes, in the following way:

> Gary: People are helpful. If you miss a lesson and you ask someone for their notes or whatever, they're not going to say 'no'.
>
> Abraham: In my class people are helpful. I find they help me loads
>
> Clark: I don't think there's been a time yet when we've been doing assignments, and man has been stuck, no-one's been turned away.

Joseph: That's the thing with assignments. When you're proper stuck, someone always helps you. If someone's behind with their work I'd go out of my way to help them.

In this scenario, the students are actively engaged in an attempt to increase their personal standing within education by striving to obtain recognised qualifications. This desire to increase status by obtaining valued qualifications is consistent with Bourdieu's construction of how individuals working to accrue cultural capital as a means of facilitating progression within education know that certain forms of capital, such as recognised education qualifications, are accorded greater status than other forms of capital such as 'street knowledge' (Ogbu, 1991:265). This understanding demonstrated Black men and boys' implicit understanding of Bourdieu's proposal that education has the capacity to 'confer capital, particularly cultural capital, upon its participants' and how such 'qualifications tend to be highly valued' (Webb, Schirato and Danaher, 2002:110) both within education and wider society beyond.

Black men and boys displayed a critical awareness that education qualifications were and are a signifier of cultural capital and that those with greater amounts of such capital were more likely to be readily accepted and successful within mainstream education and society. Most Black students possessed a deep seated, almost intuitive understanding of the importance of academic qualifications for these reasons and some Black students had an even more developed understanding of the significance of academic qualifications. Robbie and Clement in particular, who were both studying level 3 qualifications, had made the link between educational cultural capital and securing high status, well paid jobs or gaining places on higher level courses, and appreciated the link between gaining qualifications and the direct, tangible benefits such qualifications were capable of producing.

The significance of peer support was further emphasised in discussions about friendship groups. Their friends served as a key support mechanism to assist students in both their academic work and their social discourse. All students agreed that although they were at college to obtain a qualification and had plans to progress onto further study or into employment, the presence of a supportive peer group was an important feature of college life which enabled them to both enjoy being at college and to achieve their chosen qualifications.

Family support

A key support mechanism identified by all Black students was family support. Family members were seen as always willing to help another member of the family in their academic development. Research has consistently demonstrated that 'Caribbean parents were keen that their children should get ahead in school' (Figueroa and Nehaul 1999:18) and were positive advocates of academic learning – although other groups have expressed similar views. However, the importance of family support was heightened for Black students, many of whom believed schools and to some extent colleges were incapable of or unwilling to provide them with the support they needed to succeed. This has been confirmed by other research (Ogbu 1991; Fordham, 1996; Sewell 1997; Blair, 2001) which has shown that schools and White teachers in particular were unable to provide effective support for male or female Black students. Together with peer and class tutor support, Black students viewed family members as the best providers of help. Level 2 business students Barry and Issac explained:

> Barry: Family, it's just family really.
>
> SP: When things go wrong is it your mates you turn to for support?
>
> Issac: I'd probably turn to my family. Like my aunty or something, 'cause I'm pretty close to her. She's like my sister really, so I'd probably turn to her.

The potential difficulty associated with family support was that although most students' parents and other family members had been educated in the UK, many of them had experienced a negative journey through education. Consequently, they had not had the chance to develop a detailed understanding of the nuances of the system. So beyond providing emotional support, they might not have been best placed to guide Black men and boys in their journeys through schools and colleges.

When trying to decide whether family or friends were best placed to help, the students sometimes appeared to be torn:

> SP: If your mates couldn't help where else could you go for back up?
>
> Peter: Family, my Mum or my brother. It depends. If it was just in college I'd rather go for my mates first, but if it was out of college then I'd go for my family first then I'd go for friends
>
> (Level 1 sports student)

The students' deeply held beliefs regarding the nature of college support and the perceived ineffectiveness of school support cannot be easily explained. For those who took part in this study, these views were likely to have been created by a variety of factors, including the structure of the school and college curriculum, and their understanding of issues associated with race and institutional culture. However, both organisationally and culturally, colleges were significantly different from schools. Part of this difference was embedded and enacted in the way college staff behaved when working with students. The approach adopted by college staff made the support they offered more acceptable to Black students so that they in turn were more willing to accept such support. It is important to note that with the inevitable biological bonus endowed by time, the students themselves had grown up somewhat. The passage of time had given students the opportunity to reflect on their own personal goals and how these might be achieved. Their maturity may well have made it easier to acknowledge that they needed help and to accept support. This transition was summarised by a level 1 sports student, John:

> John: School life was full of shit to tell you the honest truth. That's school life – you don't know where you're going. But when you come to college you pick your course, you build a relationship with people around you, and from there that sets your mind straight on where you're going in life and what you want to do.

Other research (Channer, 1995; Blair, 2001) has shown religion to be an essential support for many Black people in their educational journeys. Channer asserted that the church 'environment gave the reinforcement needed to deal with the regular emotional and psychological 'onslaught'' (1995:106) endured in schools. She found that 'many respondents reflected on the benefits of being a church member' (*ibid*:105). Interestingly, none of the Black men and boys who engaged with my inquiry accepted this position. Even when asked a direct question about the significance of religion helping them to continue in education or to support them in focusing on their academic pursuits, none of them identified that religion was, or could be, an important support system. Indeed some actively sought to distance themselves from religion, like this level 3 student:

> Robbie: I don't believe in the church and I don't believe in any religion. I am an atheist

Barry, a level 2 business student, was one of the few students who regularly attended church. He talked about the relationship of education and the church in the following way:

> Barry: Personally I go to church and they say you can go to them, but sometimes when problems are too personal, you don't feel secure to ask them. You just keep it to yourself.

Although the views of these students may not have been representative of the whole group, they were contrary to Channer's view and challenged the notion that religion could be 'a source of strength in [the] quest for academic success' (1995:111) for all Black men and boys.

Personal agency

This section discusses how the students in my study had become self-reliant autonomous learners, driven by their own personal motivation and self-determination. It is not possible to say how widespread such personal deter-mination to succeed was among them, but other research suggests that some Black men and boys do not conform to societal expectations and have made choices 'outside the cultural milieu in which they were raised' (Noguera, 2003:440). They have found ways to assert their agency in countering negative 'structural and cultural forces' (*ibid*) such as schools which have failed to provide rewards 'commensurate with their educational efforts and accom-plishments' (Ogbu, 1991:283). In order to persist and succeed in education Black students have had to become self-supporting and rely on their own resources. As Peter and Robbie said:

> Peter: I just make the effort on my own behalf. I'm not really bothered what the college thinks of me. As long as I get my thing at the end of the year...I come here for my own benefit and to make my mum happy. Not just to make my mum happy, 'cause I'm doing it on my own behalf as well, but I want to make her happy on top of it.

> (Level 1 sports student)

> Robbie: I'm here to learn and leave. That's what I'm here for. I'm here basically to get the knowledge that is in the teacher's head into mine. That's the only thing I'm interested in.

> (Level 3 business student)

Personal motivation, although useful, was not sufficient in itself to secure success and they needed an almost blinkered bloody-mindedness to accomplish their goals. This resolute self-determination to achieve against the odds was developed by Robbie and Clement as follows:

> Clement: I've got my own determination not to fall by the wayside, and be like everyone else, and just have a normal job and work in an office. I've got a goal, and even though it might take a while to reach that and go through many steps, I think I will because this is just one of the steps I need to do.

> (A level student)

> Robbie: The only thing I believe in is myself and I can do anything that I put my mind to. Anything I want to do I know I can do it. That's how I think.

(Level 3 business student)

These comments revealed deep complexity of thought. Clement did not specify his comments related exclusively to males, so his words can be taken to apply to all Black people. Clement believed that firstly, Black people commonly fell by the wayside; secondly, that many Black people could expect no more from life than the mundane; and thirdly, that for Black people to achieve at all they could expect to go through 'many steps'. While any long term goal would probably require proceeding through numerous stages, Clement implied that even when they had ability and ambition, they could expect to take much longer than their White counterparts to achieve their goals. In their research Aymer and Okitikpi (2002) confirmed Clement's belief that opportunities for Black people were limited or curtailed. Ogbu found that Black people 'learn about the job ceiling quite early in life from observing their unemployed and underemployed parents, older siblings, relatives, family friends and other adults' (1991:280). Robbie, in contrast, still maintained an unerring sense of personal advocacy and thought his self belief would sustain him in the face of any difficulty in life and enable him to achieve all his goals and ambitions.

The employment situation for Black men has not changed substantially since Ogbu's 1991 research. A decade later, Aymer and Okitikpi found that an African-Caribbean graduate 'is more than twice as likely to be unemployed as a White person with A levels [and] African men with degrees are seven times more likely to be unemployed as White male graduates' (2002:7). Consequently, the 'persistence of racialised exclusion'(Bhavnani, 2006:83) which has kept Black people out of the employment market made Robbie's faith in his own agency appear naively optimistic. Clement's comments however, were perceptive and insightful in recognising that Black people frequently need to apply extra effort and could expect to take much longer to achieve their goals, if they did so at all. The idea of needing to be better than their White peers appears to be deeply embedded within Black culture or as one parent proclaimed in other research 'You must remember you are Black, you have to be a bit cleverer, one above them' (Maylor *et al*, 2006:63).

Whereas school had been viewed by most of this group as a hostile environment to be survived (Eggleston *et al*, 1986), college was seen as a facility that offered new opportunities to succeed. This perception is important, as it represented students taking control of their own learning and moving from a position of being directed and controlled to taking responsibility for their own actions and their life trajectory. This awareness of taking control was demonstrated by Curtis and Stephen, who were both studying level 2 art courses, and Robbie who was on a level 3 business course:

> Stephen: Basically at college you make your own decisions.
>
> Curtis: If you wanna be here, you wanna be here.
>
> Stephen: Exactly.
>
> Curtis: You've got to determine your own success.
>
> Robbie: That's where college comes in, because you're here basically, to better yourself.

By acting like this, these students had chosen to reject a Boudieusian imposed habitus in which they had to 'adjust their expectations with regard to the capital they were likely to attain in terms of the 'practical' limitations imposed on them by their place in the field' (Webb *et al*, 2002:23). Instead they had elected to try and increase their position and standing in the field by refusing to agree to the 'deep-structur[ed] cultural matrix that generate[d] self-fulfilling prophecies' and obliged them to accept 'the limited opportunities that previously existed for their success in school' (Swartz, 1997:104).

However, despite this drive to succeed and even with strong positive motivation, some students found they experienced difficulties in maintaining focus and at times simply lacked the physical energy to continue with their studies:

> John: Everybody has one of them days, don't they? Where you wake up and you just can't be bothered. You're just fed up.
>
> (Level 1 sports student)
>
> Abraham: Sometimes you just have to grit your teeth and work through it. And sometimes, I won't lie, I'm struggling to stay awake, like my head on the table and not even looking.
>
> (A level student)

These findings provide evidence that even within the context of educational marginalisation and failure in the statutory sector, numbers of Black men and boys were able to remain positive about education and be pro-education, seeing it an opportunity for career and personal advancement. This positive attitude was significant because it is contrary to the popular stereotype of Black men and boys being education resistant and low achievers. It challenges educators to provide alternative explanations for Black student disengagement within the statutory sector. One such explanation could be that Black students have endured an education system that is dismissive of their needs and believes their failure is a predicted and pre-determined outcome. Worse still, such failure could be the result of a callous and uncaring education system.

I have shown that one of the factors sustaining Black males and enabling them to persist with their studies in negative learning environments was their belief in themselves. They were able to remain within and even succeed in the system through their sheer, gritty self-determination. However, 'it would be naive and erroneous to conclude that strength of character and the possibility of individual agency [alone] can enable one to avoid the perils present within the environment' (Noguera, 2003:440). To combat these dangers a view is needed that looks afresh at issues, develops existing successful approaches and searches for new and innovative strategies that can support Black men and boys to achieve in education.

Conclusion

This chapter shows how although support mechanisms were routinely accessed and used by Black students, they can best be described as informal self-help systems which have not been formally planned and engineered but which are organic and evolutionary. These systems, while useful, might have been sufficient to meet the range of educational, social and emotional needs of Black men and boys – or they might not.

Are college organised support systems relevant for all students? Black men and boys demonstrated a systematic aversion for *all* college support systems, including academic support like literacy and numeracy workshops, as well as emotional support systems such as counselling. This situation cannot be easily explained. It may have been influenced by male pride and an unwillingness to acknowledge that they needed support, and they saw this need as a display of weakness and a challenge to their masculinity.

However, Black students who accepted emotional support claimed to feel more confident working with someone of the same racial group. Consequently the lack of Black counsellors possibly made college services appear unattractive. The unwillingness to use college counselling services could equally be explained by gender differences, as many college counsellors were, and still are, female. It was possible the Black male students were reluctant to discuss their concerns with White women. The issue of accessing college based support thus had both racial and gender features, which combined to effectively exclude Black men and boys.

As a consequence of this exclusion, Black men and boys have had to work out their own support structures and have plotted their own routes to success by a variety of means. Their other option was to leave their academic achievement to chance. Noguera, a Black male researcher, claimed that 'the only thing that spared [him] the fate of so many of [his] brethren was luck' (2003: 433). The students involved in my inquiry were unwilling to adopt such a fatalistic approach and chose instead to take positive steps to try and engineer their chances of success in education.

PART FOUR
PLANNING FOR THE FUTURE

8
Recommendations

Introduction

> If there is one concept that dominates European social policy discourse in the early years of the twenty-first century it is 'social exclusion'. It is deemed to be the principal reason why contemporary societies lack cohesion. The solution, it is suggested, lies in policies that actively promote social inclusion. This would be helpful, if it were not for the eerie silence about ... how the goals are to be achieved. (Ratcliffe, 2004:1)

If we are to embrace the challenges of the future, we need to build 'a plural community' (Potter, 2005:29). Colleges are microcosms of society and, like society, need actively to plan to include *all* communities and individuals. While not shattering Ratcliffe's 'eerie silence', this chapter identifies initiatives that would positively enhance the experience of Black men and boys' education and thus their life chances. Such initiatives are badly needed in education because some colleges have barely begun to develop 'policies for social inclusion' (Potter, 2005:29).

Although FE appears to have provided an environment which seems more suited than school to the needs of Black men and boys, encouraging their academic development, there are still many areas which require improvement. It would be easy to suggest simple, glib answers here. But this would mask the complexity of the situation and obscure the need for a multifaceted strategy which responded adequately to the challenges of the situation. When such a complicated and difficult situation has persisted for such a long time, it would at best be naively optimistic to believe there were simple solutions that could be quickly implemented. At worst, it could demonstrate a callous disregard for these young people and reveal that there was no real intention of trying to bring about change. When Coard exposed the way the system treated Black school pupils in England in 1971, the challenge was how to change the education system so that it provided for the needs of all Black pupils. While there has been progress towards achieving this aim, the challenge of producing an education system in which all learners studying in all sectors can achieve and thrive has yet to be met.

Actions to promote change
The eradication of racism

Race, racism and equality have been persistent themes in this book. However, racism evolves and changes with time and location, and the challenges encountered by one community are not necessarily the same as the issues faced by another. The issue of racism has been further complicated by those who 'believe that a colour-blind approach is the best way to end discrimination' even though 'individuals spontaneously and unconsciously categorise people by race [and] snap decisions are made' based on a person's assumed racial origin (Anderson, 2010:240). Anderson notes that 'in the context of racism, the colour-blind perspective can be used to justify inaction through denial, thereby maintaining the current power structure and preserving privileges of the dominant group' (p250) and 'the stronger the colour-blind attitudes people have the less likely they will be to support affirmative action' (*ibid*:246). And the more likely racism will persist unhindered.

Bhavnani, Mirza and Meetoo define racism in the following way:

> Racism operates along at least three axes. First it is characterised by denigratory stereotyping, hatred and violence. Second, it sets in motion cycles of disadvantage. Third, it negates and even obliterates the culture, religion and language of groups concerned. (2006:15)

Their definition does not adequately define institutional racism, however. Here, organisations work to systematically disadvantage certain groups, a process which is complicated by the prevailing 'confusion in understanding' (*ibid*:30). Bhavnani and her colleagues maintain that it is the combination of these different expressions of racism – individual, societal and institutional – that colleges need to address if they are to eliminate racism in FE.

Although most organisations and most people recognise the damage racism can do to the life chances of groups and individuals nowadays, it remains an emotive term which some people and institutions find difficult to acknowledge, and this can result in failure to confront the problem. However, the DfES suggested that 'perhaps an inflammatory term is needed to tackle the complacency and intransigence that has led to the existence of institutional racism in the education system' (2006:26) and, rather than focusing on the sensitivities of those who find racism a difficult term, it would be better for colleges to devise ways to tackle racism in the education system.

Racism remains 'a complex social reality with a long and painful history and it would be arrogant to suggest that there are any ''off-the-peg' answers' (Dadzie, 2004:ix). While 'the case for antiracism has been firmly established ... the challenge ... in the 21st century is to translate it into viable day-to-day practice', she argues, so as to ensure that Black students are not intentionally or unintentionally harmed by education. Gillborn argues that 'racism gains strength from too many quarters simply to be taught out of existence' (1995:2); answers to this complex, difficult and persistent social issue are not waiting to be found but have to be created by the efforts and energies of those committed to bringing about change and are likely to differ in different institutions. There is a moral, social, ethical and educational imperative for colleges to develop practices that will reduce and ultimately eradicate racist influences because 'the education system *does* have the potential to challenge racism in ways that may have a lasting impact on students of all ages and ethnic backgrounds' (*ibid*, original emphasis).

College tutors are a fundamental feature of college life, acting as gatekeepers to student progression and having significant influence in creating the college's culture. College staff have a key role to play in eliminating racism from the college environment. To achieve this aim colleges need to ensure that they:

- recruit staff with appropriate attitudes who are supportive of social justice and promoting change
- provide existing staff with training which supports them to work with and meet the needs of diverse client groups.

Most job descriptions for organisations in the public sector now require potential employees to show a commitment to equal opportunities and to agree to follow relevant workplace policies. Most organisations will enquire at interview if potential employees are in agreement with implementing existing equality legislation. However, not all employers pursue this point rigorously. Colleges need to find ways to explore this issue in depth and gain greater understanding of potential new staff members' commitment to equality. In-tray exercises which posed difficult and challenging scenarios and asked candidates about their past experience would help to test individual commitment. Simple, one-dimensional answers are unlikely to be useful. Candidates need to be able to explore issues from a variety of perspectives, including that of minority groups. Managers who are used to expecting model answers will also require training so they can accommodate the range of responses this approach would produce. Introducing or including exercises and questions relating to the Equality Act 2010 may extend the interview process, but investing time in recruitment and training would pay dividends in terms of the suitability of employees recruited. Colleges should consider extending Ofsted's concept of limiting grades to include employment procedures, and not appoint people who gave answers which revealed attitudes which could not be addressed effectively through training.

Existing staff should have their attitude towards and promotion of equality and diversity monitored through an appraisal process which considers information from a range of sources and that includes the students. This concept of assessment was adopted by Ofsted in its 2009 common inspection framework for FE. It introduced 'three critical judgements', including equality and diversity (Ofsted, 2009:10), which would 'contribute to and limit the grade for overall effectiveness' of a college (p19). Where 'a judgement of inadequate [was] awarded for equality and diversity, it [was] unlikely that the overall effectiveness of the provider [would] be better than satisfactory' (p21).

The 2009 guidelines were still current for colleges in 2012, although new guidelines were produced for schools. While the 2012 guidelines for schools do not include limiting grades, inspection is underpinned by a set of key principles which include 'eliminating discrimination, promoting equal opportunities and encouraging good race relations' and 'encouraging schools to meet the diverse needs of all pupils' (Ofsted, 2012:11). Employees should be assessed on how effectively they promote 'social and educational inclusion' (p19) and staff who fail to perform adequately would have their performance grade for overall effectiveness limited and would be given targets to improve.

These actions may appear draconian, but Ofsted spells out that equality and diversity in practice means:

- actively promoting positive relationships and respect for human rights
- understanding and respecting differences
- taking positive actions to tackle unlawful discrimination, inequality and unfairness
- adopting practices that make best use of the differing skills and talents of individuals

■ focusing on improving outcomes that raise standards and improve lives. (*ibid*:19-20)

This definition is wholly consistent with equality legislation (including the Race Relations Amendment Act, 2000: the Disability Discrimination Act, 2005; and the Equalities Act 2010) and LLUK's requirement that all tutors in the sector show commitment to 'equality, diversity and inclusion in relation to learners, the workforce, and the community' and 'apply principles to evaluate and develop (their) own practice in promoting equality and inclusive learning and engaging with diversity' (LLUK, 2006:3). It is also consistent with the Institute for Learning's (IfL) Single Equality Strategy which 'aspires to go beyond the legal requirements relating to equality' (IfL, 2009:3). Implementing good practice relating to equality and diversity is not an additional burden on staff or an optional extra, as under current guidelines working towards the eradication of racism is simply fulfilling the requirements of being a tutor in FE.

Once members of staff have been appointed and are in post there needs to be ongoing staff training to ensure that staff comply with their contractual and legislative obligations. To achieve this goal colleges need to provide 'proper training on race equality' (DfES, 2006:17) which recognises 'issues specific to sub-groups' (*ibid*:19) of students and staff. While it appears that in most colleges 'teachers, managers and support staff [have] benefited from some training in equality and diversity ... inspection reports suggest that there is insufficient training in about half of all colleges' (Ofsted, 2005:21). Consequently equality training remains an area for development in many colleges and training could usefully be extended to include 'a compulsory induction module on equality and diversity, run termly to ensure that all new teaching staff participate(d) early in their employment (with further) regular planned activities to raise awareness and help staff plan their work to meet the college's equality objectives' (*ibid*:21-22). An initiative of this nature would support teaching staff in working with diverse communities and could contribute towards their ongoing continuing professional development. Such an approach would certainly help to promote the equality agenda within colleges and help to ensure institutional racism became a historical artefact.

Developing a supportive institutional culture

Developing a supportive institutional culture is intrinsically linked with having members of staff who are committed to promoting equality and diversity. This applies to staffing at all levels, underpinned by a commitment from senior management to initiate and bring about institutional change. This change begins with formulating and promoting an equalities policy which caters for the needs of all current and future college clients. Worryingly, 'six per cent of colleges nationally did not have an equal opportunities policy' as recently as 2002 (Commission for Black Staff in FE, 2002:78). While it is unlikely that there are any colleges in 2012 which have no equalities policy, as all must comply with the 2010 Equality Act in order to achieve a satisfactory Ofsted report, the fact that some colleges have only recently developed policies indicates that they have much work to do to understand and implement equalities principles, policies and practice adequately.

This issue was confirmed in a 2004-05 Ofsted survey, which found that although colleges 'were broadly meeting their responsibilities under the legislation. ... too few were actively and systematically instigating change to improve race equality at the rate which might be expected ... particularly with regard to staffing and governance' (Ofsted, 2005:1). This damning indictment by Ofsted suggested a picture of widespread institutional complacency among colleges. Their managers lacked direction or a sense of urgency to promote and accelerate the equality agenda. Ofsted noted that one of the most significant factors in achieving institutional change was 'the leadership of the principal and senior managers in establishing a college-wide ethos of equality and high aspirations for all' (*ibid*). Ofsted found that leadership was underdeveloped or lacking too many colleges.

College staff at all levels, from principal and teaching staff through to administrators and maintenance staff, have a key role to play in developing a supportive institutional culture. One of the key findings of my research was Black students' belief that their tutors valued them as individuals and created an atmosphere 'where learners of diverse heritage felt welcome and safe' (Ofsted, 2005:1). Tutors did not ignore difference and were aware of and acknowledged the issues being a Black man might present in wider society. Within college, tutors made serious efforts to respect *all* students regardless of ethnicity, signalling to Black students that they were valued and included members of the college community, and were afforded the same rights and responsibilities as any other college user. This was consistent with Ofsted's findings that college students commented favourably on 'the good atmosphere of the institution' (Ofsted, 2005:25). The Black men and boys who took part in my study also reported positively on the supportive and helpful nature of college tutors and drew particular attention to the difference in attitude between their college tutors and former school teachers.

While it appears that colleges have achieved a degree of success in generating an institutional culture which is more sympathetic and supportive to the needs of Black students, this has been an organic outcome rather than a planned and systematic development. Colleges can still engage more pro-actively to advance positive race relations: the key is that they must have a systematic approach to staff training on equality issues.

Staffing issues

All the students who participated in my inquiry stated it would have been easier to form positive working relationships if their tutors were Black. And they believed this would have benefited their learning and overall experience of FE. In common with the students in Byfield's research, most Black men 'would have welcomed' (2008:81) the opportunity to work with more Black tutors because Black tutors 'helped ensure that practices ... were fair' and 'they were noted for giving Black students that extra push to maximise their potential' (p83). The appointment of more Black staff in FE would be a posi-tive step to support the learning of Black students. Unfortunately the situa-tion in the sector has been and remains less than encouraging.

Data from 2002 indicated that 'compared to White teaching staff, Black staff are under-represented at all levels. Moreover, half of all Black teaching staff (3.5%) appear[ed] to be concentrated in part-time posts' (Commission for Black Staff in FE, 2002:36). When Avril Willis, then Director of Quality and Standards at the Learning and Skills Council (LSC), was interviewed in 2002, she stated it was unacceptable that 'the only Black people [students] may en-counter were auxiliary staff'. This prompted her to set a target 'to see 11 Black principals in the sector by 2009' (Black Staff Commission News, 2002:2). Sadly, 'whilst some organisations in the public sector had set themselves time-related outcomes (ie. 'goals') ... over half of respondents from the educa-tion sector had not identified outcomes' for improvement (Commission for Racial Equality, 2003:6).

The number of Black staff in FE had not risen significantly by 2005. Trevor Phillips, then Chairman of the Commission for Racial Equality and now of the Equality and Human Rights Commission, 'warned that colleges could have compliance orders placed on them to force them to recruit and promote more Black and ethnic-minority staff' (Clancy, 2005, *TES* online). Unlike the US, UK legislation does not apply a quota system in employing Black people. While Phillips suggested that compliance orders *could* be used to encourage colleges to employ more Black teachers, he said, in the same interview, 'We don't want to do that do we? It would be much better if the sector wakes up and makes an effort'. Thus he left the responsibility for employing more Black tutors with the colleges. To date no specific agency or individual has shown the will to compel colleges to take more affirmative action.

Despite the lack of positive action and the weak targets (if any) being set by education organisations, there have been some improvements in employment since Phillips's remarks. The overall figure of Black teaching staff employed in the sector fell from 7 per cent in 2002 to 6.5 per cent in 2005-06, but by 2009 eleven Black and ethnic minority principals were employed in the sector, thus meeting 'the target set by the Learning and Skills Council in 2002' and it was claimed that 'each one [was] mentoring several senior staff from minority backgrounds supporting and encouraging them as they prepare[d] for principalship' (Thomson, 2009, *TES* online). This has been a significant achievement and 'while 11 Black and ethnic minority principals does not sound much and is only 3 per cent of the total, it is more than there has ever been' (*ibid*). Moreover, the mentoring arrangements that have been established provide a mechanism to increase the number of Black principals and managers in the future.

For there to be greater representation of Black staff at all levels within colleges, 'there is undoubtedly much more to be done' (Commission for Black Staff in FE, 2004:2). There will have to be a 'commitment from the top if equality and diversity are to be effectively mainstreamed' (*ibid*:12).

Promoting their own success

It would be easy to construct Black men and boys as the powerless victims of an oppressive regime, who have little choice about how they interact and interface with the education system. However, to present such a picture would fail to respect to the students themselves. hooks claims that Black males are 'groomed to be without choice' (2004:35) by the dominant hegemony, but this view may accord more power than is appropriate to the education system. While not minimising the significant structural inequalities within education, it would nonetheless be inaccurate to claim that Black males have no influence on their own lives. Black boys and men have choices and though some appear to believe that 'no matter how hard they work they would not rise up' (Datnow and Cooper, 2008:191) and conform to the stereotype of underachieving lost causes, there are those who realise that 'embracing the stereotype could be life-threatening' (hooks, 2004:35) and instead choose to 'educate themselves within educational systems that [are] not supportive' (*ibid*) of their needs and still become 'actively engaged in the creation of their own academic success' (Datnow and Cooper, 2008:206).

Steele highlights a critical factor when he asserts that:

> school achievement depends, most centrally, on identifying with school; that is forming a relationship between oneself and the domains of schooling such that one's self regard significantly depends on achievement in those domains. (Steele, 2008:167)

While some Black men have worked tirelessly to 'acquire education on all levels' (hooks, 2004:33), others 'have given up on the system' (Majors and Billson, 1992:7) and rejected mainstream education as a way of expressing their masculinity. This rejection mirrors Willis' 1977 research findings that White working class youth 'resisted school and created their own standards for measuring success' (Datnow and Cooper, 2008:191). For Black men and boys to work within education requires them to value 'school achievement in the sense of its being a part of one's self-definition' (Steele, 2008:165). Black men need to believe that rather than being instruments of oppression, education and learning can be useful mechanisms of liberation and advancement. In short, it is necessary for Black men and boys to believe that education is cool.

Black men need to redefine cool 'to include academic success' (Datnow and Cooper, 2008:205) and to 'develop academic identities without feeling as though they [are] diminishing their cultural identities' (*ibid*, 2008:193). Zepke, Leach and Butler observed that 'self-determination [was] enhanced where supportive social-contextual conditions exist to promote feelings of self efficacy' (2010:4). If such conditions could be successfully established in colleges then Black men and boys would be enabled to make positive choices about their education. Bourdieu's notion of habitus creating a self-fulfilling prophecy would not apply because they would use their personal agency to promote a positive academic outcome.

Opportunities for colleges and schools to build systems to support Black men

Although colleges have recognised that 'support for learners, both personal and academic, is an important aspect of the promotion of equality of opportunity' (Ofsted, 2005:22) in compliance with their duty under the 2010 Equality Act, it has not been clear how colleges have worked to meet learners' cultural and emotional needs and colleges appear to have struggled to take appropriate action to promote positive race relations. Even though the need for further action has been identified by both Ofsted and colleges, there has been a notable lack of action in this area.

Providing an organised and systematic approach to capturing learner voice could help develop a more supportive institutional culture for Black students. Learners themselves can tell colleges how best to support their needs because, as consumers, they are ideally placed to 'find a creative solution' (Hanman, 2005:171) to persistent issues. Most colleges have an active student union or a student council which works to engage with the student population and to represent their views to college management. However, many college student unions/councils adopt a homogenous approach to student voice, viewing them as a single collective body and not always recognising difference. It may be more appropriate for FE colleges to consider the model adopted in many HEIs and to have separate union officers who bring together 'group[s] of similarly situated people and give them the time ... to talk through their everyday life, reflect on that and get ideas from each other' so they can begin to 'make positive changes' to systems and structures (Morrison, 2008: 17). 'Regular monthly or termly meetings [could] be arranged' where Black men and boys met together to discuss pertinent issues (Malik, 2000:641). In this way the distinct voices of different groups, such as mature learners, women students, students with disabilities and Black students are captured, preserved and represented.

While there is still an issue with organising along these lines, in that it appears to assume that the needs of all Black, women, mature or disabled students are the same, there is at least a distinct vehicle for bringing the views of these different interest groups to the fore. Students have explained how helpful they found it to be with their Black peers and how being with them enabled them to articulate their views on learning and other education issues. It appears that Black males understand what it is they require to support their learning and can identify ways to achieve success, but they need support in forming groups which can interface with college tutors and managers to express these ideas.

While there would be distinct positive advantages in forming and recognising Black male student support groups, there may be inherent difficulties in establishing such groups. Would Black students be willing to join them? Would they use the group constructively to raise issues of concern? Would it be representative of the college's Black male student population? Would colleges be willing to support groups of this type? Who would co-ordinate it? Could such a group become an instrument of hegemonic control or perceived as such? While there may be difficulties in setting up Black male student support groups, they could become a valuable conduit between students, college tutors and management. If colleges were to take the significant step of routinely establishing this type of student support group, which had direct dialogue with college management, this one action would support colleges in achieving their equality objectives and could potentially help to accelerate the improvement of race equality. Essentially, colleges need to start implementing the mantra that 'young people are part of the solution, not the problem' (Alexander and Potter, 2005:198).

9

Conclusions and challenges

Introduction

Although part of the mainstream education system, FE both positions and prides itself as a different offer to secondary school and HE. It has attracted uncomplimentary labels from government – Sir Andrew Foster called it 'the neglected middle child' (2005). Some learners too have shown ambivalence towards the sector. While appearing keen to participate in college programmes, they have come to view FE as the 'last chance saloon' for students of all ages who may have either left school with few or no qualifications or indeed have rather chequered school or learning histories', operating on the margins of mainstream provision (Salisbury and Jephcote, 2008: 151). However, FE's peripheral position has given the sector certain freedoms and even though it often operates in a climate of extreme uncertainty the FE sector has, to a degree, been able to retain and develop its own unique identity which separates it from secondary education and the HE sector (Kelly, 1992; Vella, 1994; Fieldhouse, 1998; Bhattacharyya *et al*, 2003).

The eclectic nature of FE appears to make it ideally suited to support students who have experienced 'low expectations' (Morrison, 2010:75) in their previous learning environments. In common with other groups who are presented as educationally disadvantaged (for example working-class people, refugees and late returners to study), Black men and boys have appreciated 'the more relaxed, less rigid college timetable', 'the availability of free time', 'the use of first names with college teachers' and the lack of 'petty rules and less regimentation' (Salisbury and Jephcote, 2008:154).

It was this difference which was so enjoyed by the students who participated in my inquiry, particularly those who had undergone bruising learning ex-

119

periences in other education sectors. Released from the imposition of strict 'controlling environments' (*ibid*) and damaging stereotypical perceptions of them so prevalent in the secondary sector, Black boys and men have been able to use FE to re-enter education and access mainstream opportunities from which they had previously been excluded. Thus FE has promoted their effective 're-engagement with education' (Attwood, Croll and Hamilton, 2004: 111).

Key findings of the research
The FE curriculum

FE succeeded in providing a very different curriculum from schools. The students could access choices which were not routinely available elsewhere and an environment in which it was accepted 'that adults or, more specifically, non-graduate adults can make sensible decisions for themselves' (Wolf, 2010:20). This was particularly significant for Black students who, while in school, often had academic and curriculum choices made for them, frequently based on 'societal ... and negative stereotypes about their abilities' (Steele, 2008:164). Because many Black men and boys did not 'fit in with the dominant cultural values perpetuated through the school system' (Byfield, 2008:13), they had repeatedly been placed into lower streams where their opportunities were limited and their chances of progression restricted.

On entering FE students had some influence over their curricula choices, often for the first time, and were enthusiastic about being treated as adults capable of making 'good choices for themselves' (Wolf, 2010:21). They had 'clear ideas about what they were interested in, and about where their self interest' lay (*ibid*). In FE Black students were able to construct a curriculum based primarily on *their* choice rather than on institutional direction. This was a strongly motivating feature of studying at college and links well with ideas of personalised learning, where students are supported to construct a curriculum which is relevant to their individualised needs.

Although the relative academic freedom was a positive feature of college, it also held a potential danger. Black male students are rarely presented as academic or well motivated but portrayed instead as being part of a 'laddish culture of boys that disparage academic work' (Byfield, 2008:47). They are popularly accepted as having particular talent at sport, music and performing arts and many appear to gravitate to these areas by choice. While some individuals may be suited to studying these subjects, tutors who are willing to accept the stereotypical view of their abilities may inappropriately direct Black learners to these areas, thus limiting their opportunities to study more traditionally academic disciplines (Sewell, 2004; Youdell, 2004; Steele, 2008). Many of those in my study had chosen to study sport and in some ways fulfilled stereotypical expectations about their abilities. But others who took part in the inquiry had made different choices including business, art and A-levels and, critically, no-one believed they had been compelled to make certain typical choices about what to study.

The findings from my research indicated that FE was successful in its aspiration of providing a different curriculum offer and creating a more inclusive culture which was respectful towards and met the needs of Black men and boys. This was in direct contrast to many Black students' experience of schools where they reported encountering 'direct racism, either from pupils or teachers' (Ritchie, 2010:28) and feared discriminatory treatment because of their ethnicity. Racism had been exacerbated by apparent willingness of some schools' to ignore the 'openly racist attitudes among pupils' (Ghouri, 1999, *TES* online) and the 'racist bullying' (Bloom, 2009a, *TES* online) to the extent that policy on 'race-related education and equality in schools has been a litany of 'broken promises''(Bloom, 2009b, *TES* online). In contrast, colleges have made positive progress in managing race related incidents and Ofsted found that they have 'sound processes for receiving learners' complaints and analysing them' (2005:11).

Support in FE

Relevant, timely support was a key feature for the Black students who had a positive learning experience and achieved academic success (Blair, 2001; Rhamie, 2007; Byfield, 2008; Sewell, 2009). This was echoed in the findings of my research. Appropriate support was crucial in enabling Black males to feel part of the college community.

The assistance given by the college staff was a critical feature of these support networks. The students who took part in my inquiry understood the inherent power balance within the education system and they appreciated how their academic achievement could be, or had been, influenced by teachers who acted as gatekeepers to their academic success. Some of the research participants had had experienced at first-hand negative 'differential treatment' (Byfield, 2008:39) or had been victims of the 'low expectations' (*ibid*:38) held by their school teachers. The students in my study were not looking for special favours from the college but wished merely to participate on an equal footing with their White peers and were aware of the difference their tutors could make to their progression. Unlike their White peers, however, many Black students needed to regain confidence in an education system that had previously failed them and had to build positive student/staff relationships when they entered FE. They were now having to risk putting their trust in education again.

'Good interpersonal relationships between teachers and pupils are funda-mental to successful teaching and learning' for all students (Byfield, 2008:80), but these relationships were even more significant for those who had had a negative school experience. In the case of the Black men and boys in my study, positive student /tutor relationships were more likely to succeed when the students believed that the staff genuinely cared about them. This could even mean the tutor 'assuming the role of ... surrogate parent' (Humphrys, 2010:2) because the students needed to believe that their tutors held their 'best interests at heart' (Byfield, 2008:85) and could 'lock down the destructive instincts that exist within all males' (Sewell, 2009:33). Lewis, a Black lecturer in one of the colleges in my study, provided such a role model for Black men and boys, pressuring them to do well while making it clear he was doing this to encourage them and help them reach their potential. Although he was initially 'uncomfortable in this role' Lewis, like Sewell, chose to maintain this persona 'because the boys seemed to like it' (2009:31). Not only did they wel-come this role modelling but the tutor provided the structure and discipline they needed to help them achieve their academic goals. This was in sharp contrast to the school teachers who operated an environment in which Black students were 'disrespected, talked down to, over-monitored, blamed for things they did not do, and given no chance to tell their side of the story' (Byfield, 2008:80).

The issue of mentors directly employed, and so controlled, by the school or college is a sensitive one. Although student mentors 'received official approval when they were introduced into British schools through the UK Government's *Excellence in Cities* policy in 1999' (Russell, 2009:57) and have 'been particularly successful' (Majors, Wilkinson and Gulam, 2003:208) in supporting learning in some school and colleges, none of the students who participated in my research had been involved in formal mentoring relation-ships. Although they would have positively welcomed the opportunity to work with Black male staff, they did not specifically identify the need for a Black male mentor. They readily turned to college tutors who 'took a personal interest in them, encouraged them, were friendly towards them, treated them equally and provided them with opportunities to excel' (Byfield, 2008:81). These features characterise classic mentoring relationships (Clutterbuck and Megginson, 2005; Wallace and Gravells, 2007). The Black men and boys iden-tified tutors who possessed these skills intuitively and gravitated towards them. Thus they effectively identified tutors who were capable of providing mentoring support 'as part of an organically evolved strategy' (Majors, Wilkinson and Gulam, 2003:211). This apparently eliminated, or at least minimised, the need for a formally designated mentor and suggests that Black men and boys are best placed to identify solutions to the issues they face.

Peer support

To complement the support they received from the staff, all the students in my inquiry utilised peer support and friendship groups to help them navigate the education system. They used their peer group as a mechanism of 'positive action and control', rather than engaging in a 'cathartic expression of frustrated power and social maladjustment' (Wright, Standen and Patel, 2010:83). Sewell also found that peer support assisted learners to overcome obstacles. He relates how a secondary tutor directed a 'bright and disciplined boy ... to take an 'unruly' student under his care and supervision, whereupon complaints about his bad behaviour diminished significantly' (2009:115). The students intuitively understood what was needed to help peers refocus their energies in a positive manner.

Building on this premise, some schools have introduced learner support groups to allow students 'space to talk' as a way of helping them to manage their academic and personal concerns. The ultimate goal is to enable the students to move to a position of 'giving each other advice' (Morrison, 2008:13-14). Students are in a unique position to offer support to their peers: they have had similar experiences and share a common understanding. While students may not be the voice of academia or authority, they *are* the authentic voice of experience and perhaps understand more than anyone else how it feels to be a Black student in the British education system today. And what is more, they have the advantage of not only knowing *what* needs to be said but also *how* it should be expressed. The challenge for all phases of the education system, schools, universities *and* colleges is to determine how this experience can be harnessed so that the learners are enabled to use each other as a source of support in their decision making and progression through education. This should not be left to chance and luck,.

Family support

The students in my study recognised the significant support they received from their home environment and found their families to be a particular source of strength, 'acting as a site of support and nourishment for the development of positive and healthy identities' (Wright, Standen and Patel,

2010:60) and consistently demonstrating a willingness to be actively involved 'in their sons' education' (Byfield, 2008:139). They echoed the findings of Mirza in that they 'derive[d] much of their determination for 'getting on' from their parental orientation and both the passive and active support this engendered' (2009:15).

However, families that digress from 'the traditional classic ... nuclear family ... of the father who is head of the household and economic provider; the mother who is the homemaker and provides domestic care and socialises the children, and the helpless and dependent children whose emotional, financial and welfare needs are met by their parents' are in danger of being viewed as abnormal (Wright, Standen and Patel, 2010:60).

This presents a particular difficulty for Black students because the 'idea that a Black child can be brought up and nurtured in an isolated nuclear family is historically an alien concept to many African and Caribbean families' (*Black Parent Network,* online). While the idea of the nuclear family appears to maintain popular currency – especially among certain religious fundamentalist groups, the tabloid press and traditional Conservative politicians – it is rapidly becoming a historic concept which does not fully reflect the way families are constituted in the UK today.

The 2001 UK census showed 'just under one in ten households in England and Wales [were] lone-parent (9.6%)' with 'an increasing proportion of children born outside of marriage' and 'around half of Black Caribbean (48%) and Other Black (52%) households with dependent children were headed by a lone parent. The percentage for the White British group was 22%' (National Statistics, online). Within this context, the Black population may be presented as 'problematic and undesirable... and when difficulties emerge, they themselves are blamed and punished' for choosing to adopt a different family organisation to the idealised nuclear family (Wright, Standen and Patel, 2010: 60). Put more crudely, the failure of Black youth in education is constructed as a situation which 'classically dysfunctional' Black families have brought on themselves through inadequate parenting of their sons (Mirza, 2009:55).

Such a narrow view, however, does not adequately accommodate or recognise the extended nature of the Black extended family, which is:

> a multigenerational, interdependent kinship system which is welded together by a sense of obligation to relatives ... and has a built in mutual aid system for the welfare of its members and the maintenance of the family as a whole. (Martin and Martin, 1978:1)

Within a well developed and socially accepted kinship system, being a lone parent is not necessarily a problem, as families can rely on the support of a network of relatives in fulfilling the duties of parenting. This positive construction of the Black family unit is rarely recognised and the efforts of many Black families who 'have done and are doing an excellent job in difficult circumstances to support their children' (*Black Parent Network*, online) seldom receive acknowledgement. This has not been the case for all Black families, however. In some urban areas extended family networks have been replaced in children's lives by gangs. These 'are the new extended families' for a worrying number of young Black people, offering the attention and support traditionally given by family members (Umunna, 2007, online). Although peers may be a helpful source of guidance and support, if the prevailing value system is that of the gang and is based on anti-social behaviour and violence it is likely to lead to problems such as school failure and criminality.

Academic achievement

The academic underachievement of Black male students in education is complex. Describing students as 'Black' can be unhelpful in this instance, as it masks significant factors such as socio-economic status, parental occupation, gender and nationality. Similarly, describing students as 'White' does not adequately describe the many factors that combine to influence student achievement. Unravelling these different factors, which appear to be linked in various ways, is an on-going challenge. However, it is clear that race is a significant and persistent feature in the academic achievement of Black men and boys.

National test data collected in the UK for key stage 1 (age 5-7) key stage 3 (age 11-14) and first public exam sittings (age 16) reveal that 'the mean scores of Black African, Black Caribbean (and) Black Other are below the mean for White British peers' (Strand, 2010:2). Although it is accepted that at all key stages 'White boys from poorer socio-economic backgrounds achieve lower … than any other main group' (Weston, 2010:1) and appear to be 'particularly vulnerable to low parental social class' (Strand, 2008:2), Strand's 2010 findings confirm that Black students are still at risk of underachieving relative to the majority of their peers of all ethnicities. According to this view, Black student achievement remains a cause for concern. White boys from poor backgrounds appear to be especially susceptible to low academic achievement, but Gillborn's analysis produces a very different interpretation of the same data. He argues:

the data shows that, far from the picture of White failure generated by media coverage of the statistics, White non-FSM [free-school meals] students – of both sexes – are more likely to succeed than their peers from Pakistani, Black Caribbean, Black African, Black Other and Dual Heritage (White/Black Caribbean) backgrounds. (Gillborn, 2008:56)

Gillborn makes the case that although there is low achievement by White working class boys, to highlight this one feature ignores 'non-FSM students [who] form the great majority of the cohort (86.6 per cent of the young people)' (2008:55). It thus gives a distorted picture of academic achievement across the sample, directing attention away from Black underachievement across all socio-economic groups, back towards the White majority.

Ofsted has recognised the need to address ongoing achievement issues across different groups within the statutory sector. 'In the new Ofsted framework there is a key focus on the achievement of any vulnerable group' (Weston, 2010:1). In the framework White working class boys and *all* Black boys (regardless of their social positioning) should be considered priority groups for attention. Unfortunately Ofsted and government agencies have failed to identify how such persistent underachievement could be addressed or what positive intervention strategies are needed.

While there are continuing issues relating to academic achievement for Black students in the statutory sector, this picture seems not to be mirrored in FE, in terms of both academic outcome and experience (see *The FE curriculum* earlier in this chapter). The National Audit Office reported that there had been 'a substantial improvement in recent years' (National Audit Office, 2001: 2) in the number of students successfully completing college courses, so that from 1994 to 1999, achievement rates rose from 65 per cent to 74 per cent' (*ibid*:15). More recent benchmarking data compiled by the LSC indicated that 'the upward trend in learner achievement [had] been sustained across all types of FE provider and across all notional NVQ levels of learning aim' (LSC, 2006, online). Furthermore:

> success rates of learners from ethnic minorities in 2004/05 have all shown increases of between 1 and 3 percentage points compared to 2003/04. Black African, Black Caribbean and Chinese ethnic groups have all shown the greatest improvement in success rates and in each of these groups, success rates for males have increased more than for females. (*ibid*)

Placed in the context of the types of learners who attend college courses, for example those who have achieved no qualifications, adult returners, as well as those who have had challenging learning experiences, this represents a significant achievement. This was echoed by the findings of my research: all the students in my inquiry were successful in achieving their primary learning outcome. Considering that some of those who participated in my study had been excluded from their secondary schools, the importance of achieving in FE becomes even more profound and FE appears to have found ways to support many different learners, including Black men and boys, in realising their educational goals.

Potential challenges

The previous chapter identified some strategies to enhance the educational experience of Black men and boys as they navigated their way through FE. These included:

- eradicating racism
- developing a supportive institutional culture
- recruiting suitable staff members and providing appropriate training
- supporting learners to utilise their personal agency in a positive fashion, and
- building relevant support systems.

Each of these on its own has the potential to make a difference to Black boys and men as they move through the FE sector. Collectively they present an opportunity to change the way that the FE sector responds to educating Black male students. Regrettably, few if any of these suggestions have been adopted in a systematic fashion in colleges to date, even though many are relatively low cost ideas and would not require significant capital investment.

But to implement these changes demands determination from all the college staff, from principals to premises officers, to question and confront existing structures and systems and to search for new ways of working. This is a significant challenge. Unless tutors, managers and others who work within the FE sector demonstrate the resolve needed to transform learning and usher in a new era characterised by equality and fairness, opportunities to achieve wholesale change within the sector will not be realised. Unless and until the hearts and minds of all staff are won over, any changes are likely to be superficial and short lived. They will be of little value if they are driven only by a need to comply with external or internal directives or legislation rather than by a genuine consensus that new ways of working are needed.

Like all public sector organisations, colleges are obliged to function within a legislative framework. Being publically funded, they are ultimately responsible to the government to promote and achieve key government objectives. This used to mean that colleges were obliged to meet the requirements of the Race Relations (1976) and the Race Relations Amendment (2000) Acts and to publish statements on how they would work to promote positive race relations. The Equality Act 2010, which replaced all previous equality legislation, claims to 'bring together; harmonise and in some respects extend the current equality law' and is intended to 'remove inconsistencies and make it easier for people to understand and comply with' legislation (Government Equalities Office, 2010:3-4). The Equality Act is intended 'to help tackle discrimination and inequality' (*ibid*) and is designed by central Government policy to support educational institutions to promote equality and challenge all forms of unfairness.

However, the merging of separate, discrete Acts including the Race Relations Acts, the Disability Discrimination Act and the Sex Discrimination Act into a single Act, may have the effect of weakening responses to promoting race equality, rather than strengthening equality legislation. As late as November 2010, as the Equality Bill was being progressed through Parliament, Race on the Agenda (ROTA) which is 'one of Britain's leading social policy think-tanks focusing on issues that affect Black, Asian and minority ethnic communities' expressed its concerns that the Bill was 'not fit for purpose' and declared its uncertainty as to how the Bill would support organisations to 'actually take action to promote equality' (ROTA, online). ROTA was concerned that 'in the absence of more prescriptive duties' and because the Act 'carries no stipulation that public bodies set Equality Objectives for each protected characteristic' some organisations might choose not to identify the promotion of positive race relations as a priority. Accordingly, ROTA believed that the Equality Act, rather than strengthening equality legislation was 'a regression from the existing consultation duty under the Race Relations (Amendment) Act 2000' and rather than benefiting Black groups was actually a barrier to achieving positive change within colleges (*ibid*).

The recently introduced raising of the participation age so that 'by 2015 all young people will continue in education or training to 18' (DCSF, 2009:26) is a further threat to implementing positive change to support the education of Black men and boys in colleges. Although there are various options available to 16-18 year olds, including sixth form colleges, apprenticeships and employment with accredited training, it is reasonable to predict that many of the young people who are now obliged by law to remain within education or training will continue their education in FE colleges. This initiative has the potential to change the population of learners who attend college, moving it from an elective client group who have chosen to participate (see Chapter 3) to a part-conscript population. This significantly changes the way colleges recruit students and may have a profound impact on the culture of colleges. It may even make some of the features of college life which Black men and boys found helpful and positive disappear under the pressure colleges will face to find ways to accommodate learners who would not have chosen to remain in education.

Colleges are not islands. They are part of the wider community. They are not removed from local communities, but operate within and are part of them, working with industries and services to try and meet the needs of the various communities they serve. As colleges try to minimise the effect of government imposed threats to achieving change, they may find that they become more reliant on community networks. And it is these networks that will be part of a collective solution to meet the needs of Black men and boys and other disadvantaged learners.

Conclusion

I have used this final chapter to summarise the key findings of my inquiry so as to anticipate the challenges for the future. FE remains a constantly evolving and dynamic environment that seeks to cater for a very diverse client group.

The education of Black men and boys in the UK is complicated by different and sometimes contradictory features. What may appear to be a positive development for one community or a single individual may be less than satisfactory for another. But this does not suggest that certain approaches or ideas are invalid or should not be tried or re-tried. The responses that may be required to help improve the educational journey of Black men and boys in FE are situated in specific conditions. There is unlikely to be one simple, quick-fix approach which would improve academic achievement and enhance the learning experience of Black boys. It is incumbent on the education community and others committed to promoting educational equality to keep trying to develop new and different ideas to overcome difficult and deep seated situations. Not all the ideas will work, but that does not justify ceasing to try. In spite of earlier setbacks and difficulties many Black students remain positive about education and they return to FE even after disappointments, to try and attain the academic qualifications they could not achieve in secondary school. At the very least, the education system should recognise and respond to this persistence and seek to support learners in their efforts to achieve. Ultimately the education system will need to learn to work with Black learners to produce a new, responsive, effective and fair system.

It is simplistic to assert that colleges usually get it right and schools usually get it wrong. But the differences between the way the two sectors function have had, and continue to exert, a profound effect on the experiences of Black students. This has led them to form quite different opinions of the two sectors. More research is needed to establish that the experiences reported by the cohort in my research are widely applicable to Black boys and men at schools and college. But the findings of my research have important implications for the practices of FE colleges and equally powerful implications for schools.

Appendix 1
Individual interview schedule

Following the focus group sessions, selected students were invited to take part in individual interviews to further explore issues raised in the group sessions. All students were asked the same core ten questions shown below:

1. Where in college would you say your social space is? Why?

2. When you socialise in college who do you choose to associate with? Why? Does race or gender influence your choice of groups you mix with?

3. As you move about college do you perceive you are treated differently in any way because of your ethnicity? If so how does this manifest itself? How does it make you feel?

4. Do you experience different treatment from different staff groups – refectory, library, reception, academic etc?

5. Do you believe your race has any impact on the way staff treat/perceive you?

6. Have you ever experienced an aspect of the curriculum as hostile towards you – eg. through omission or racist representation?

7. How welcoming do you feel the physical environment of the college is to Black males?

8. What internal support mechanisms are available to you in college?

9. Have any other support mechanisms (eg. church, family) been important to you during your time at college?

10. In what ways do you feel the college demonstrates it values you?

Appendix 2
Focus Group Prompts to Facilitate Discussion

Participants were given a series of grids and envelopes containing possible descriptions of the feature they were asked to discuss. The prompt words and phrases are set out below. Participants had to agree which descriptions they would use. They were free to add new descriptions if they felt the choices they had been given were inadequate. Participants were free to complete the grids in any order.

Grid 1: I would describe college as ...

boring, dull, too strict, cold and damp, stupid, a waste of time, weird, not complicated, friendly, happy, interesting, laid back, warm, a good laugh, shit, better than a crap job

Grid 2: The atmosphere in college is ...

boring, dull, too strict, crap, stupid, harsh, hostile, friendly, happy, interesting, laid back, warm, good, shit, easy-going

Grid 3: The best/worst thing about college is ...

my mates, the canteen, being able to smoke, the lessons, rules, getting a grant, late finishes, girls, the teachers, the library, wearing what I like, the way I'm treated, free lessons, choosing what I study, early finishes

Grid 4: The attitudes of students towards each other is ...

friendly, caring, considerate, open, honest, sound, helpful, mean, angry, snidey, bitchy, snobby, stuck-up

Grid 5: The behaviour of students towards each other is ...

fresh, friendly, arrogant, easy-going, stupid, supportive, bad, aggressive, not complicated, laid back, cocky, good, ok

Grid 6: Staff at college ...

have it in for me and my mates, have their favourites, praise me if I do well, pick me if I volunteer, care about me, overlook me to answer questions, ask before judging, try their best to be fair, speak to me aggressively, prefer the girls, speak to me like an adult, listen to my side, reprimand me more harshly than others, jump to conclusions, give me a chance to join In, have high expectations of me, blame me first, take an interest in me, give me a chance, have low expectations of me, believe in my abilities, couldn't care less about me

Grid 7: The college curriculum is ...

relevant, meaningful, good, stimulating, interesting, varied, stupid, pointless, dull, boring, meaningless, too samey,

Glossary

BBC	British Broadcasting Corporation
BME	Black and Minority Ethnic
CSE	Certificate of Secondary Education
DCSF	Department of Children Schools and Families
DES	Department of Education and Science
DfEE	Department for Education and Employment
DfES	Department for Education and Skills
FE	Further Education
FEU	Further Education Unit
GFE	General Further Education
GCSE	General Certificate of Secondary Education
HMI	Her Majesty's Inspectorate
LSC	Learning and Skills Council
NIACE	National Institute of Adult and Continuing Education
NUT	National Union of Teachers
Ofsted	Office for Standards in Education
O-level	Ordinary Level
SEN	Special Educational Needs
SFA	Skills Funding Agency
UK	United Kingdom
YCS	Youth Consult Survey

References

Aldridge, F and Tuckett, A (2003) *Light and Shade*, Leicester: NIACE

Alexander, T and Potter, J (2005) Manifesto: Education for Change, in *Education for a Change*, Alexander, T and Potter, J (eds) London: RoutlegeFalmer

Allen, G (2006) Is Discrimination De-motivating? The case of Black Caribbean boys and girls, BERA Annual Conference 2006

American Statistical Association (ASA) (1997) *What Are Focus Groups?* available at http://www. webpages.uidaho.edu~redgeman/Sampling%20PDF%20Files/focusgroups.pdf accessed 10 January 2008

Anderson, K J (2010) *Benign Bigotry, The Psychology of Subtle Prejudice*, Cambridge: Cambridge University Press

Angelou, M (2001) *I Know Why the Caged Bird Sings*, Bury St Edmunds:The Folio Society

Angelou, M cited in Kelly, B (2003) *Worth Repeating More*, Grand Rapids: Kregel Publication

Attwood, G, Croll, P and Hamilton, J (2004) Challenging Students in Further Education: themes arising from a study of innovative FE provision for excluded and disaffected young people, *Journal of Further and Higher Education*, 28(1) pp109-119

Aymer, C And Okitipi, T (2002) *Young Black Men and the Connexions Service*, DfES Research Brlef 3 I I

Bagley, B and Coard, B (1975) Cultural Knowledge and Rejection of Ethnic Identity in West Indian Children, in *Race and Education Across Cultures*, Verma G K and Bagley, B (eds), London: Heinemann

Baker, M (2002) *Educational Achievement*, available at http://news.bbc.co.uk/hi/english/static/in_depth/uk/2002/race/educational_achievement.stm accessed 16 July 2007

Bartlett, S And Burton, D (2007) *Introduction to Education Studies*, 2nd edition, London: Sage

BBC News (2003) Summit on Black Pupils' Results Crisis, available at http://newsvote.bbc.co.uk./mpapps/pagetools/print/news/bbc.co.uk/1/hi/education/301 Accessed 11 September 2004

BBC News (2011) African-Caribbean Boys' Would Rather Hustle than Learn', available at http://newsvote.bbc.co.uk/news/education-153874444?print=true Accessed 17 November 2011

Bhattacharyya, G, Ison, L and Blair, M (2003) *Minority Ethnic Attainment and Participation in Education and Training*, Nottingham: DfES Publications

Bhavnani, R, Mirza, H and Meetoo, V (2006) *Tackling the Roots of Racism: lessons for success*, Bristol: Policy Press

Black Parent Network, Parenting Issues, Black Family, available at http://www.blackparentnetworl.com/parents/blackfamilycontents.dwt accessed 17 October 2010

Black Staff Commission News, September 2002, Issue 4, Tunbridge Wells: Commission for Black Staff in FE

Blair, M (2001) *Why Pick On Me? exclusion and Black youth*, Stoke on Trent: Trentham Books

Blair, M And Bourne, J (1998) *Making the Difference: teaching and learning strategies in successful multi-ethnic schools,* Norwich: The Open University and DfEE

Bloom, A (2009a) Racial Equality Failed by '12 Years of Labour's Broken Promises', *Times Educational Supplement*, 9 October, available at http://tes.co.uk/article.aspx?storycode=6012264 accessed 9 October 2010

Bloom, A (2009b) Racist Bullying Rife in Schools, Says Poll, *Times Educational Supplement,* 24 April, available at http://tes.co.uk/article.aspx?storycode=6024638 accessed 30 January 2010

Brighouse, H, Tooley, J and Howe, K R (2010) *Educational Equality,* London: Continuum

Byfield, C (2008) *Black Boys Can Make It: how they overcome obstacles to university in the UK and USA*, Stoke on Trent: Trentham

Cantor, L, Roberts, I and Pratley, B (1995) *A Guide to Further Education in England and Wales*, London: Cassell Education

Cassidy, B (2005) Black Boys Do Better, available at http://www.independent.co.uk/news/education/education-news/black-boys-do-better-486348.html accessed 23 March 2008

Centre for Social Justice (2009) *Dying to Belong: an in-depth review of street gangs in Britain*, London: Centre for Social Justice

Channer, Y (1995) *I Am A Promise: the school achievement of British African Caribbeans*, Stoke on Trent: Trentham Books

Charmaz, K and Mitchell Jr, R G (1997) The Myth of Silent Authorship: self, substance and style in ethnographic writing, in *Reflexivity and Voice*, Hertz, R (ed), London:Sage

Clancy, J (2005) Recruit Black Staff 'Or Else', *Times Educational Supplement*, 28 January, available at http://tes.co.uk/article.aspx?storycode=2069053 accessed 30 December 2010

Clough, P (2002) *Narratives and Fictions in Educational Research*, Buckingham: Open University Press

Clutterbuck, D and Megginson, D (2005) *Techniques for Coaching and Mentoring*, Oxford: Elsevier Butterworth-Heinemann

Coard, B (1971) *How the West Indian Child is Made Educationally Subnormal in the British School System,* London: New Beacon Books

Commission for Black Staff in FE (2002) *Challenging Racism: FE leading the way*, London: Commission for Black Staff in FE

Commission for Black Staff in FE (2004) *Race Equality in FE Employment: the Commission's legacy,* London: Commission for Black Staff in FE

Commission for Racial Equality (2003) *Towards Racial Equality: an evaluation of the public duty to promote race equality and good race relations in England and Wales (2002)*, London: Commission for Racial Equality and Schneider-Ross

Connor, M K (2003) *What is Cool: understanding Black manhood in America*, Chicago: Adgate

Coventry University *Focus Groups*, available at http://www.corporate.coventry.ac.uk/cms/jsp/polo poly.jsp?d=2929&a=18163 accessed 31 December 2007

Dadzie, S (2004) *Toolkit for Tackling Racism in Schools*, Stoke on Trent: Trentham Books

Datnow, A and Cooper, R (2008) Peer Networks of African American Students in Independent Schools: affirming academic success and racial identity, in *Foundations of Critical Race Theory in Education*, Taylor, E, Gillborn, D and Ladson-Billings, G, (eds), London: Routledge

Department for Children, Schools and Families (2009) *14-19 Briefing: making change happen, notebooks schools version*, London: DCSF

Department for Children, Schools and Families (2010) Statistical First Release: key stage 4 attainment by pupil characteristics, in England 2008/09, available at http://www.dcsf.gov.uk/rgateway/DB/SFR/s00900?SFR_2009Revised.pdf accessed 20 March 2010

Department for Education (2010) Equality Act 2010: advice for school leaders, school staff, governing bodies and local authorities, available at http://media.education.gov.uk/assets/files/pdf/e/equality%20act%20guidance%20december%202011.pdf accessed 27 February 2012

Department for Education (2011) Raising the Participation Age (RPA), available at http://www.education.gov.uk/16to19/participation/rpa accessed 29 May 2011

Department for Education and Skills (2005) *14-19 Education and Skills*, Annesley: DfES Publications

Department for Education and Skills (2006) *Getting It, Getting It Right*, No Location:DfES

Department for Education and Skills (2007) *Gender and Education – the evidence of pupils in England,* Annesley: DfES Publications

Dhillon, J K, McGowan, M and Wang, H (2008) How Effective are Institutional and Departmental Systems of Student Support? insights from an investigation into the support available to students at one English university, *Research in Post-Compulsory Education*, 13(3), pp281-293

Eggleston, J, Dunn, D, Anjal, M and Wright, C (1986) *Education for Some*, Stoke on Trent: Trentham Books

Ely, M Vinz, R Downing, M and Anzul, M (1997) *On Writing Qualitative Research, Living by Words*, London: Falmer Press

Farsi, S S (1981) *Swahili Sayings 1*, Dar es Salaam: East Africa Publications

Fieldhouse, R (1998) *A History of Modern British Adult Education*, Leicester: NIACE

Figueroa, P and Nehaul, K (1999) Parenting and Academic Achievement: Black pupils, Black parents and Schooling, BERA Annual Conference 1999

Fordham, S (1996) *Blacked Out, Dilemmas of Race, Identity and Success at Capital High*, Chicago: University of Chicago Press

Fordham, S and Ogbu, J (1986) Black Students' School Success: Coping With the Burden of Acting White, *Urban Review*, 18(3), pp 176-204

Foster, A (2005) *Realising the Potential: a review of the future role of FE colleges*, Nottingham:DfES

Frankel, A and Reeves, F (1996) *The Further Education Curriculum in England: an introduction,* Bilston: Bilston College Publications

Further Education Unit (1985) *The College Does It Better*, Portsmouth: Further Education Unit/Eyre and Spottiswoode Ltd

Further Education Unit (1987) *Black Perspectives on FE Provision – a summary document,* Coventry: Further Education Unit

Fyfe, A and Figueroa, P (1993) *Education for Cultural Diversity – the challenge of a new era,* London: Routledge

Garner, R L (2006) Humor in Pedagogy: how ha-ha can lead to ah-ha, *College Teaching*, 54(1), pp177-180

Ghouri, N (1999) Schools Ignore Issue of Racism, *Times Educational Supplement*, 26 February, available at http://tes.co.uk/article.aspx?storycode=313809 accessed 23 August 2010

Gibbs, A (1997) Focus Groups, *Social Research Update*, University of Surrey, 19(4) available at http://sru.soc.surrey.ac.uk/SRU19.html accessed 15 January 2008

Gidman, J, McIntosh, A, Melling, K and Smith, D (2011) Student Perceptions of Support in Practice, *Nurse Education in Practice*, 11 pp351-355

Gillborn, D (1995) *Racism and Antiracism in Real Schools*, Buckingham: Open University Press

Gillborn, D (2008) *Racism and Education: coincidence or conspiracy?* Abingdon: Routledge.

Gillborn, D and Mirza, H (2003) *Educational Inequality, Mapping Race, Class and Gender: a synthesis of research evidence*, London: Ofsted

Government Equalities Office (2010) *Equality Act 2010; What Do I Need to Know? a summary guide for public sector organisations*, London: HMSO

Golden, S, O'Donnell, L, Benton, T and Rudd, P (2005) *Evaluation of Increased Flexibility for 14-16 Year Olds Programme:outcomes for the first cohort*, Nottingham: DfES

Grant, P (1992) Using Special Education to Destroy Black Boys, *Journal of Negro Education*, 43(1-2) pp17-21

Green, A and Lucas, N (2000) *FE and Lifelong Learning: realigning the sector for the twenty-first century,* London: Institute of Education

Griffiths, M (1998) *Educational Research for Social Justice: getting off the fence*, Buckingham: Open University Press

Gutteridge, R (2001) Student Support, Guidance and Retention: re-defining additional needs, Coventry University: Qualitative Evidence-Based Practice Conference

Hall, R E (2005) Eurocentrism in Social Work: from race to identity across the lifespan as biracial alternative, *Journal of Social Work*, 5(1) pp101-114

Hall, V (1994) *Further Education in the United Kingdom*, London: Collins Educational

Hanman, D (2005) Listen to Students, in *Education for a Change*, Alexander, T and Potter, J (eds) London: RoutlegeFalmer

Henderson, A T and Mapp, K L (2002) *A New Wave of Evidence: the impact of school, family and community connections on student achievement*, Texas: Southwest Educational Development Laboratory

Henn, M, Weinstein, M and Foard, N (2006) *A Short Introduction to Social Research*, London: Sage

hooks, b (1994) *Teaching To Transgress*, New York: Routledge

hooks, b (2001) *Salvation, Black People and Love*, New York: William Morrow

hooks, b (2004) *We Real Cool, Men and Masculinity*, New York: Routledge

Humphrys. J (2010) Why Our Schools Need Big Heads, *The Sunday Times*, Section 4 *News Review*, 19th September 2010, pp1-3

IfL, (2009) Draft Single Equalities Strategy, available at http://www.ifl.ac.uk/_data/assets/pdf_file/0015/9312/Single-Equality-Strategy-Consultation-Copy-2.pdf accessed 31 October 2010

Jacklin, A and Le Riche, P (2009) Reconceptualising Student Support: from 'support' to 'supportive', *Studies in Higher Education*, 34(7), pp735-749

Jarvis, P (2005) Human Learning: the interrelationship of the individual and social structures, in Jarvis, P and Parker, S. (2005) *Human Learning, An Holistic Approach*, London: Routledge

Jensen, R (2011) Whiteness, in *The Routledge Companion to Race and Ethnicity*, Caliendo, S M and McIlwain, C D (eds), London: Routledge

John G (5 April, 2010) A Stretch Too Far for the Tories, available at http://www.guardian.co.uk/commentisfree/2010/apr/05/extra-schooling-education-gap accessed 26 February, 2011

Jones, M, Siraj-Blatchford, J and Ashcroft, K (1997) *Researching into Student Learning and Support in Colleges and Universities*, London: Routledge and KoganPage

Kelly, T (1992) *A History of Adult Education in Great Britain from the Middle Ages to the Twentieth Century,* Liverpool: Liverpool University Press

Kher, N, Molstad, S and Donohue, R (1999) Using Humor in the College Classroom to Enhance Teaching Effectiveness in 'Dread Courses', *College Student Journal*, 33(3), pp400-406

Kincheloe, J L (1991) *Teachers as Researchers: qualitative inquiry as a path to empowerment*, London: Falmer Press

Korobkin, D (1988) Humor in the Classroom: considerations and strategies, *College Teaching*, 36, pp154-158

Lee,V E, Smith, J B, Perry, T E and Smylie, M A (1999) *Social Support, Academic Press and Student Achievement: a view from the middle grades in Chicago*, Chicago: The Chicago Annenberg Challenge

Lee-Tarver, A (2006) A Survey of Teachers' Perceptions of the Function and Purpose of Student Support Teams, *Education*, 126(3) pp525-533

Levy, A (2010) *The Long Song*, London, Headline Publishing Group

Liamputtong, P (2007) *Researching the Vulnerable: a guide to sensitive research methods,* London: Sage

LLUK, (2006) *New Overarching Professional Standards for Teachers, Tutors and Trainers in the Lifelong Learning Sector,* London: LLUK

London Development Agency (2004) *The Educational Experiences and Achievements of Black Boys in London Schools 2000-2003: a report by the Education Commission, London*, London: Development Agency

LSC (2006) *Benchmarking Data 2002/03 to 2004/05*, http://readingroom/lsc.gov.uk/lsc/National/Benchmarking0405.pdf accessed 26 October 2010

Lucas, N (2004) *Teaching in Further Education*, London: Institute of Education

Mac an Ghaill, M (1988) *Young Gifted and Black*, Milton Keynes: Open University Press

Majors, R, and Billson, J M (1992) *Cool Pose: the dilemmas of Black manhood in America*, New York: Lexington Books

Majors, R, Wilkinson, V and Gulam, W (2003) Mentoring Black Males: responding to the crisis in education and social alienation, in *Educating Our Black Children – New Directions and Radical Approaches*, Majors, R. (ed) London: RoutlegeFalmer

Malik, K (2008) *Strange Fruit: why both sides are wrong in the race debate*, Oxford: One World

Malik, S (2000) Students, Tutors and Relationships: the ingredients of a successful student support scheme, *Medical Education*, 34, pp635-641

Martin, E P and Martin, J M (1978) *The Black Extended Family*, Chicago: University of Chicago Press

Maylor, U, Ross, A, Rollock, N and Williams, K (2006) *Black Teachers in London*, London: Greater London Authority

Mendoza-Denton, R and Downey, G (2002) Sensitivity to Status Based Rejection: implications for African American students' college experience, *Journal of Personality and Social Psychology,* 83(4) pp896-918

Miles, M B and Huberman, M (1994) *Qualitative Data Analysis*, London: Sage

Miller, J and Glassner, B (1998) The 'Inside' and the Outside': finding realities in interviews, in *Qualitative Research, Theory, Method and Practice*, Silverman, D (ed), London: Sage

Mirza, H (2009) *Race, Gender and Educational Desire: why Black women succeed and fail*, London: Routledge

Mitchell, C (2011) *Doing Visual Research*, London: Sage

Morrison, A (2010) 'I Want an Education': two case studies of working-class ambition in further and higher education, *Research in Post-Compulsory Education*, 15(1), p67-80

Morrison, N (2008) Ready to Talk, *Times Educational Supplement Magazine*, 9 May

Muraskin, L (1997) *'Best Practices' in Student Support Services: a study of five exemplary sites*, Maryland: Westat Inc

National Audit Office (2001) *Improving Student Performance: how English further education colleges can improve student retention and achievement,* London: The Stationery Office

National Statistics Office, Census 2001- Families of England and Wales, available at http://www.statistics.gov.uk/census2001/profiles/commentaries/family.asp accessed 3 October 2010

Nehusi, K and Gosling, D (2001) Travellers' Tales from the University of East London: The Experience of 'Black' Adult Learners, Scutrea 31st Annual Conference 2001

Nelson, K J, Quinn, C, Marrington, A and Clarke, J A (2012) Good Practice for Enhancing the Engagement and Success of Commencing Students, *Higher Education*, 63, pp83-96

Noguera, P A (2003) The Trouble with Black Boys: the role and influence of environmental and cultural factors on the academic performance of African American males, *Urban Education Journal*, 38(4) pp431-459

Ofsted (1999) *Raising the Attainment of Minority Ethnic Pupils: school and LEA response,* London: Ofsted

Ofsted (2002) *Achievement of Black Caribbean Pupils: good practice in secondary school,* London: Ofsted

Ofsted (2005) *Race Equality in Further Education: a report by HMI*, London: Ofsted

Ofsted (2009) *Ofsted Inspects:a framework for all Ofsted inspection and regulations*, London: Ofsted

Ofsted (2012) *The Framework for School Inspection*, Manchester: Ofsted

Ogbu, A (1991) Low School Performances as an Adaptation: the case of Blacks in Stockton California, in *Minority Status and Schooling: A Comparative Study of Immigrant and Involuntary Migrants*, Gibson, A and Ogbu, U (eds), New York: Garland

Ouseley, H (2008) Foreword, in Byfield, C *Black Boys Can Make It: how they overcome obstacles to university in the UK and USA*, Stoke on Trent: Trentham

Petty, G (2004) *Teaching Today: a practical guide*, Cheltenham: Nelson Thornes

Phelps, R E, Taylor, J D and Gerard, P A (2001) Cultural Mistrust, Ethnic Identity, Racial Identity and Self Esteem, *Journal of Counselling and Development*, 79(1), pp 209-216

Polite, V C (1994) The Method in the Madness: African American males, avoidance schooling and chaos theory, *The Journal of Negro Education,* 63(4), pp 588-601

Potter, J. (2005) Time for Change, in *Education for a Change*, Alexander, T and Potter, J (eds) London: RoutlegeFalmer

Punch, K F (2005) *Introduction to Social Research, Quantitative and Qualitative Approaches*, London: Sage

Qualifications and Curriculum Authority (2007) *The National Curriculum: statutory requirements for key stages 3 and 4,* London: DCSF

Ram, M (1996) Ethnography, Ethnicity and Work: unpacking the West Midlands clothing industry, in *Methodological Imaginations*, Lyon, E S and Busfield, J (eds), London: Macmillan Press Ltd

Rampton, A (1981) *West Indian Children in Our Schools: interim report of the Committee of Inquiry into the education of children from ethnic minority groups*, London: HMSO

Ratcliffe, P (2004) *'Race', Ethnicity and Difference: imagining the inclusive society*, Maidenhead: Open University Press

Ritchie, M (2010) Learning to Believe, *TES Magazine,* 24 September 2010, pp27-29

Rhamie, J (2007) *Eagles Who Soar: how Black learners find the path to success*, Stoke on Trent: Trentham

Rhamie, J and Hallam, S (2002) An Investigation into African-Caribbean Success in the UK, Race, *Ethnicity and Education,* 5(2), pp 151-170

Rollock, D A, Westman, J S and Johnson, C (1992) A Black Student Support Group on a Predominantly White University Campus: issues for counselors and therapists, *The Journal for Specialists in Group Work*, 17(4) pp243-252

ROTA (Race on the Agenda) (2010) *Response to the Government Equalities Office Specific Duties Consultation on behalf of the ROTA-led Winning the Race Coalition*, available at http://www.roat.org.uk/Downloads/Response%20to%20the%20Government%20Equlaities%Office%20Specific%20Duties%20Consultation%20ROTA%20and%20Winning%20the%20Race.pdf accessed 21 February, 2011

Rowntree, W J and Binns, H B (1985) *A History of the Adult School Movement*, Nottingham: University of Nottingham Department of Adult Education

Rubenstein, D and Simon, B (1973) *The Evolution of the Comprehensive School,* London: Routledge and Kegan Paul

Russell, M (2009) Towards More confident Learners: the use of academic mentors with foundation degree students, *Research in Post-Compulsory Education*, 14(1), pp57-74

Salisbury, A and Jephcote, M (2008) Initial Encounters of an FE Kind, *Research in Post-Compulsory Education*, 13(2) p149-162

Schensul, S L, Schensul, J and LeCompte, M D (1999) *Essential Ethnographic Methods*, California: Altamira Press

Scott, D and Usher, R (1999) *Researching Education: data, methods and theory in educational inquiry,* London: Continuum

Sewell, T (1997) *Black Masculinities and Schooling: how Black boys survive modern schooling*, Stoke on Trent: Trentham Books

Sewell, T (2004) Loose Canons, Exploding the Myth of the 'Black Macho' Lad, in Manifesto: Education for Change, in *The RoutledgeFalmer Reader in Multicultural Education*, Ladson-Billings, G and Gillborn, D (eds) Abingdon: RoutlegeFalmer

Sewell, T (2009) *Generating Genius: Black boys in search of love, ritual and schooling*, Stoke on Trent: Trentham Books

Solorzano, D Ceja, M and Yosso, T (2000) Critical Race Theory, Racial Microaggressions and Campus Racial Climate: the experience of African American college students, *Journal of Negro Education* 69(1/2), pp60-73

Steele, C M (2008) A Threat in the Air: how stereotypes shape intellectual identity and performance, in *Foundations of Critical Race Theory in Education*, Taylor, E, Gillborn, D. and Ladson-Billings, G, (eds), London: Routledge

Strand, S (2008) *Minority Ethnic Pupils in the Longitudinal Study of Young People in England: extension report on performance in public examinations at age 16, research report DCSF No RR029*. London: DSCF

Strand, S (2010) The Limits of Social Class in Explaining Ethnic Gaps in Educational Attainment, British Educational Research Journal, 29 March 2010 (iFirst) pp1-33

Swann, M (1985) *Education for All: the report of the Committee of Inquiry into the education of children from ethnic minority groups*, London: HMSO

Swanson, D P, Cunningham, M and Spencer, M B (2003) Black Males' Structural Conditions, Achievement Patterns, Normative Needs and 'Opportunities', *Urban Education*, 38(5), pp608-633

Swartz, D (1997) *Culture and Power*, Chicago: University of Chicago Press

Teachernet, *Pupil Concentration Spans*, available at http://teachernet.gov.uk/supplyteachers/detail.cfm?&vid=4&cid=15&sid=91&ssid=4010402&opt=sectionfocus accessed 22 March 2008

Terzi, L (2008) *Justice and Equality in Education – a capability perspective on disability and special educational needs*, London: Continuum

Thomson, A (2009) Hurdles to Promotion are Letting Minority Ethnic Talents Fall Away, *Times Educational Supplement*, 8 May, available at http://tes.co.uk/article.aspx?storycode=6013009 accessed 30 December 2010

Thomson, P (2008) Children and Young\People: voices in visual research, in *Doing Visual Research with Children and Young People*, Thomson, P (ed), London: Routledge

Tikly, L, Haynes, J, Caballero, C, Hill, J and Gillborn, D (2006) *Evaluation of Aiming High: African Caribbean Achievement Project*, Nottingham: DfES

Torok, S E, McMorris, R F and Lin, W-C (2004) Is Humor an Appreciated Teaching Tool? perceptions of professors' teaching styles and use of humor, *College Teaching*, 52(1) pp14-20

Umunna, C (2007) *In Our Inner Cities, Gangs are the New Extended Families*, available at http://www.guardian.co.uk/commentisfree/2007/aug/09/comment.society/print accessed 17 October 2010

Vella, J (1994) *Learning to Listen, Learning to Teach*, San Francisco: Jossey Bass

Verma, G K and Bagley, C (1983) *Self Concept, Achievement and Multicultural Education*, London: Macmillan Press

Wallace, S and Gravells, J (2007) *Mentoring in the Lifelong Learning Sector*, Exeter: Learning Matters

Webb, J, Schirato, T and Danaher, G (2002) *Understanding Bourdieu*, London: Sage

Weston, D (2010) Raising Boys' Attainment, *Primary Headship*, 71(April), pp1-3

Westwood, S (1989) *Ethnicity, State and Nation: issues for comparative adult education*, Scutrea Annual Conference Proceedings, 1989

White-Hood, M (1994) Pride, Heritage and Self-Worth: keys to African-American male achievement, *Schools in the Middle*, 3(4) pp29-30

Wickline, V B (2003) *Ethnic Differences in the Self Esteem/Academic Achievement Relationship: a meta-analysis*, American Psychological Association Annual Conference, 2003

Wolf, A (2010) Shifting Power to the Learner, *Adults Learning*, April 2010, pp20-22

Woods, P (1976) Having a Laugh, in *The Process of Schooling, a Sociological Reader*, Hammersley, M and Woods, P (eds), London: The Open University

Wright, C, Standen, P and Patel, T (2010) *Black Youth Matters*, Abingdon: Routledge

Wright, C, Weekes, D, McGlaughin, A and Webb, D (1998) Masculinised Discourses within Education and the Construction of Black Male Identities Among African Caribbean Youth, *British Journal of Sociology of Education*, 19(1), pp75-87

Youdell, D (2004) Identity Traps or How Black Students Fail: the interactions between biographical, sub-cultural and learner identities, in *The RoutledgFalmer Reader in Multicultural Education*, Ladson-Billings, G and Gillborn, D, (eds), Buckingham: RoutledgFalmer

Zepke, N, Leach, L and Butler, P (2010) Engagement in Post-Compulsory Education: students' motivation and action, *Research in Post-Compulsory Education*, 15(1) pp1-17

Index